By Tyler Perry

Don't Make a Black Woman Take Off Her Earrings
Higher Is Waiting

Higher Is Waiting

Higher
Is Waiting

TYLER PERRY

Spiegel & Grau

New York

Published in the United States by Spiegel & Grau,
an imprint of Random House,
a division of Penguin Random House LLC, New York.

SPIEGEL & GRAU and Design is a registered trademark of
Penguin Random House LLC.

LIBRARY OF CONGRESS CATALOGING-IN-PUBLICATION DATA
Names: Perry, Tyler, author.
Title: Higher is waiting / Tyler Perry.
Description: New York : Spiegel & Grau, 2017.
Identifiers: LCCN 2017034266| ISBN 9780812989342 |
ISBN 9780812989366 (ebook)
Subjects: LCSH: Perry, Tyler. | Christian biography—United States.
Classification: LCC BR1725.P4523 A3 2017 | DDC 277.3/083092 [B]
—dc23
LC record available at https://lccn.loc.gov/2017034266

Printed in the United States of America on acid-free paper

randomhousebooks.com
spiegelandgrau.com

2 4 6 8 9 7 5 3 1

First Edition

Book design by Virginia Norey

For Aman.

My son and sun,

upbeat of my heart and healer of my soul.

What is faith? Mamma, what is faith?
Baby, faith is what you believe when you can't see.
But ain't that lying to yourself?

Contents

PART THREE

Branching Out   93

PART FOUR

Harvesting the Fruit   141

Introduction

EVER SINCE I was a little boy I've known there was
something greater than myself: something bigger,
something stronger—something higher. This holy force
was protecting me, loving me, and keeping me close. It was
helping me live through physical pain and emotional heartache, and guiding me to envision and believe in extraordinary possibilities despite all the challenges I faced in my life.
It was revealing insights into the connection of all souls. It
was pointing to the generosity and beauty of nature's gifts.
It was offering unyielding hope. It gave me faith so strong
that nothing, no human being nor horrendous event, could
destroy it. This inner knowledge and strength was as real to
me when I was a child as my own breath.

Today I know, without a doubt, that what I was experiencing then, and what I continue to experience now, is the
essence, power, and grace of God. There is no other expla-
nation for the ways in which my life has unfolded and the
ways it continues to grow.

Over the years, whenever a connection rang a bell and
stirred my soul—whether to help sort through a problem,
make a move in a particular direction, offer thanks and grat-

itude, adjust my perspective, honor a mentor, embrace forgiveness, bolster resolve, release a desire, let go of anger, help another soul, or enable me to reach higher and manifest a dream—I've tried to find the time to sit quietly, contemplate, and meditate on the lessons I learned. Once the message ripened and was clear, I would write this new awareness into a cherished leather-bound journal. *Higher Is Waiting,* composed over a ten-year period, is a collection of these insights, inspirations, and life lessons.

Higher is divided into four sections that revolve around the metaphor of a tree. I would ask you to consider it, as I do, the "Tree of Life." It describes the various stages of spiritual growth from my early childhood years to the present. I've titled the sections "Planting the Seeds," "Nourishing the Roots," "Branching Out," and "Harvesting the Fruit." The climb through these four stages has led me to higher, and the ascendency continues ever upward. With faith and grace, I believe, the sky is limitless. That's the truth for me—and it's the truth for you.

It is my hope that as you read this book, it will spark God within you and ignite a flame that makes you feel like you can go higher; know higher is waiting; understand that higher is not only a place in your thoughts, your finances, your love, and your compassion, but that it is waiting in every single aspect of your life, on every step of your journey. My hope is that these readings elevate you to a new level in *all* areas of your life.

I also wrote this book thinking about all the people in my life whom I love dearly and who struggle with love, loss, financial difficulties, disappointment, frustration, anger, and forgiveness, and who yearn for a better life for themselves and their children. My hope is that the lessons in *Higher Is Waiting,* along with God's words in the Bible, can be of service to them.

What I know about the Bible is this: Those whom God helped to ascend to a higher place were all flawed individuals, except for Jesus. They had made mistakes. Some had done terrible things and yet were still able to find their way to higher.

From kings to Moses, and Paul to Peter, when you consider all these biblical figures and their life struggles, you'll see God was right there with them. He took those souls with life's most damning issues and led them to higher. Being aware of this comforted me as a child and still does to this day. It told me that even though I am human, and have made my share of mistakes, gotten lost, and taken the wrong turn, my very humanness could not destroy the life that God was creating for me. Once I accepted this truth, I was able to go higher.

That's why I'm hoping that, as you read this book, you'll know that no matter how you see your life now—whether it's rolling along in greatness or flawed and feeling heavy and burdened with mistakes—no matter who you are, no matter what you were born into, or where you came from, there is a higher place we can all reach, one where we can achieve our greater potential. Higher isn't for just one special person; it's for everyone. It's for all of humanity. It's for all souls who open their minds and their hearts to receiving.

Higher is waiting for everyone.

PART ONE

Planting the Seeds

MY CHILDHOOD WAS A STORY of discouragement, belittlement, and unthinkable abuse, and yet I rose above. There was no way I could have found any kind of happiness, hope, or vision if my mother, Maxine, and my aunt Mae hadn't shown me the grace of God. They, as well as other powerful souls, were my spiritual role models. They didn't have great mansions or millions of dollars to leave me when they passed, but they planted the seeds of grace, the invaluable gift of knowing God.

As I look back over my early years and as I walk along my path today, I am grateful for those seeds planted in my childhood. From their powerful inspiration grew my unshakable desire to keep reaching higher and my devotion to help all people do the same.

1

Learning God Is in Control

BY THE TIME Fridays rolled around I was itching like poison ivy to get as far away as I could from Edgar P. Harney Elementary School. It was especially agonizing knowing Mamma was parked right outside waiting to drive us straight to heaven on earth—Aunt Mae's house in Greensburg, Louisiana.

Sometimes life travels a complicated route, as it did with Aunt Mae and our family. Mae was really a sort of adopted grandmother, but that information didn't get to my ears until I was older. I say "adopted" because my father, Emmitt, was abandoned and discovered in a drainage canal at the age of two. He was taken to Mae so that she could raise him. What an extraordinary sign of fate's fierce power, considering that Mae was only fourteen years old at the time. Years later this extraordinary soul helped save me, too. In Aunt Mae's presence I could breathe deeply in the sanctuary of nature, the freedom of unconditional love, and the benevolence of God's embrace.

Lucky for me we went to Aunt Mae's a couple of weekends every month and also during summer vacations. Emmitt came along with us in the summer. Ordinarily, that would have meant living in anxiety and fear, but my father was a different kind of man when he was around Mae. Instead of boiling up in anger and violence, he was a placid lake. He would even brag about what a fine son I was and about our happy life in New Orleans. Never mind that he beat and belittled Mamma and me all the time, that lies poured out of his mouth like fine grains of sand from a golden sieve.

But Emmitt wouldn't be joining us this weekend, and I just couldn't wait to be with Aunt Mae. Every few minutes I'd be checking the classroom's wall clock, tapping my pencil on the desk, or sliding my sneakers on the wood floor. When our principal finally ended the torture by ringing the copper dismissal bell, I joined the rush of fourth graders grabbing books and papers and breaking through the school's double doors to hit the sunshine.

New Orleans summers are a hot and humid mess, and the thick air can feel like a heavy-handed slap against your face. Standing outside on the school steps, I'd take a minute to catch my breath and get my bearings. Once I'd hear the familiar honk of my mother's car horn I'd fix my gaze through the sun's glare.

There she was: Mamma in her 1969 powder blue Cadillac Coupe DeVille, waving out the window. Sometimes I could see the weight of the world in her face. Today, though, Mamma's radiating her thousand-watt smile, and her joy makes me feel carefree. Knowing she's happy and my green suitcase with the metal snaps is packed for the weekend and locked in the trunk means all is right with the world.

When I reach the car Mamma leans over and swings open the passenger door. I slide in and settle down on the roomy, hot-as-a-radiator vinyl seat. She's wearing one of her usual outfits, jeans and a cotton floral blouse, her café au lait skin glistening in the heat. I'd watched her set her hair in rollers the night before and now it's brushed forward in a "push do." Mamma isn't flashy; she doesn't have to be. She never wears much makeup because she's a natural beauty. I always thought my four aunts were jealous because Mamma's the sister that God gave knock-your-socks-off looks. She's the one turning heads.

"Ready to go? Did you pee, Junior?" she asks, flashing another smile.

"Yes, ma'am," I say. I hadn't, but didn't want to take time before hitting the road.

Mamma doesn't waste another minute, either. She turns the ignition key, guns the gas pedal, and we're off. We head out to I-10 then onto I-55, leaving New Orleans behind us. Once we are free from the city, she turns up the volume on the eight-track player in the dashboard and belts out the blues, singing along with Z. Z. Hill, Denise LaSalle, and Betty Wright. I don't join in but quietly set the lyrics like an easy poem into my memory.

I also know our route to Aunt Mae's by heart. We ride along a vast bridge called the Bonnet Carré Spillway that takes us across the murky waters of Lake Pontchartrain. I stretch my arm out the window and let the steamy breeze cup my palm. Even though I've never seen an ocean, I think this must be what one looks like: water everywhere with no end in sight, big waves sloshing back and forth.

"Mamma," I say, spurred by a sudden sense of wariness. "Just look at *all* that water."

"Yeah, baby," she says.

"Why don't it overflow and cover the bridge, Mamma?"

"Because, baby, God's got it in its banks. He's in control. He's in control of the water. He's in control of the sky, and the birds, and you and me . . . and God is good, baby," she says.

"God is good."

Mamma's words settle deep in my heart: *God's got it in its banks. He's in control.*

My fear disappears like so much dust in the breeze. Now I can settle back in the vinyl seat, feel the warm wind and sunshine pressing against my skin, and simply watch the world unfold.

• Surrendering doesn't mean giving up or not caring. It means trusting and allowing things to be tended to by God. When have you done this in your life? What happened?

• When you don't surrender, what keeps you from letting go of control and trusting that God has you covered?

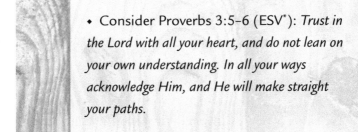

- Consider Proverbs 3:5–6 (ESV*): *Trust in the Lord with all your heart, and do not lean on your own understanding. In all your ways acknowledge Him, and He will make straight your paths.*

---

* English Standard Version

2

Talking to Jesus

TO HELP MAKE time fly, I count the trees as we speed by on our way to Aunt Mae's. When they're rushing faster and faster and I can no longer keep up, I know we're getting close. The "Amite City" sign is our exit, and once we turn off the interstate we enter a whole new world, one with no concrete sidewalks, no buildings higher than one single story, only one or two red lights, and miles and miles of open land.

There's a Kentucky Fried Chicken, and that's where we stop for a quick bathroom break and, of course, a meal of chicken, biscuits, mashed potatoes, and creamy gravy. Our stomachs full, we hit the road again. The sun is lower in the sky, but dusk has yet to cast its fading shadows. About ten miles later the Cadillac glides over a steep hill, and for miles and miles there are only red dirt roads and fields planted with cotton, sugar cane, soybeans, wheat, corn, sweet potatoes, and acres of strawberries. Two more turns and at last, at the end of a rock-pocked road, I see Aunt Mae's place.

It was obvious to me even as a child that her house had

been through tough times. Whether it was because of fierce storms or seasons of neglect, it was battered and worn-out. The wood frame was covered with some sort of material that appeared from a distance to be brick, but up close was thick slabs of gray-colored asphalt shingle, probably mixed with asbestos; the roof was rusted tin, and the whole structure tilted dramatically to one side. I had the thought "One day this raggedy old house is going to fall to the ground."

As soon as Aunt Mae hears our car pull up, the screen door snaps open and she appears with arms stretched wide like angel wings. She runs into the fenced-in front yard, shoos away the chickens and any other critters underfoot, unlatches the rickety gate, and makes her way to us as fast as her skinny legs can travel. She gets me in her grasp, squeezes me close, and cries out, "Lord, my children are here. My children are home."

It's true I was big for my age, but even at ten years old, Aunt Mae still had to reach up to hold me because she was a tiny woman, maybe no more than five foot three inches, as delicate looking as a China doll. Mae was thin and exquisite with high cheekbones, brilliant gray eyes, and shoulder-length gray hair. Her face never showed a wrinkle. She looked like she was part Native American. She had an odd fashion sense. I still wonder to this day why Mae wore so many clothes even during the summer's heat. There she is, standing under the sweltering sun, her petite frame completely covered in a long-sleeved blouse, skirt, apron, *and* pants, staring up at me with God's love in her eyes and offering the healing power of touch, all under a heap of fabric.

With our arms still wrapped around each other, we

climb the shaky front steps up to the wood porch and walk through the screen door into the living room. These were far from fancy digs. This house was one story high, only four rooms in all, with windows made of a wavy kind of old glass, and worn pine boards on the floor. Black-and-white newspaper comics were stuffed into the holes in the walls to keep the warmth or cold away. I loved the faces in the comics, but I learned at a young age that if I tried to pull them out, my hand would get slapped.

We walked straight into a small living room, maybe only 10 × 10, where Mae's grandfather, whom we called Papa Rod, would be in his bed. There was also a sofa, a chair, and a chest. Mae had a lot of chests in her small house, and every one was filled with carefully folded quilts and blankets she had sewn herself. Pictures of Martin Luther King, Jr., and John and Bobby Kennedy hung on the wall.

My aunt had things I had never seen before, like an old washing machine on the back porch where you fed clothes through the wringer. One time I got my hand caught in it and the pain shot straight from my arm into my brain. I never did that again. There wasn't any indoor plumbing, either, just an outhouse, and in the cold winter months, a lone fireplace barely kept the chill out. But who cared? I was made comfortable by the sweet power of Aunt Mae's wide smile and open heart.

Friday and Saturday nights were full of laughter and stories. Some Sunday mornings we went to church, but unlike in New Orleans, where we never missed a Sunday sermon, at Mae's we didn't go to church regularly. On one of these mornings when we weren't hurrying out, the aroma of strongly brewed coffee and freshly baked teacakes gives me a lazy wake-up call. From my cozy bed, I hear Aunt Mae singing gospel hymns:

> Precious Lord, take my hand,
> Lead me on,
> Let me stand.
> I am tired,
> I am weak,
> I am worn.

In my little-boy mind, I didn't know what Mae was singing about; all I knew was that I loved the sound of her sweet, soulful voice. On this memorable morning, I creep out of bed and without saying a word tiptoe into the kitchen and listen to Mae's singing. I'm not sure if she knows I am spying on her, but if she does, she waits a few minutes before greeting me.

"Good morning, baby."

"What you doing, Aunt Mae?" I ask in my still sleepy voice.

"Talking to Jesus, baby."

"How can you do that?"

"Did you say your prayers last night?"

"Yes, ma'am."

"Then you were talking to Jesus, too," Aunt Mae says, with her bright eyes and that orange slice of a grin.

My heart feels heavy but in a good way. Aunt Mae plants a seed inside my heart and pats it down with her loving words. I know something sacred is going to grow there.

Jesus made Mamma and Aunt Mae happy, and now I want to know Him for myself. The season of my yearning for God has arrived.

- What was the first spiritual seed that was planted in your soul?

- Recall a time in your childhood when a friend or relative helped to change you in an important way.

- Consider 1 Corinthians 3:6 (ESV):
I planted, Apollos watered, but God gave the growth.

3

Asking

COMPARED TO THE light-filled, loving times I had with Aunt Mae, weekends spent in New Orleans were doomed to turn dark and grim. On Fridays my father, Emmitt, would come home from work and walk through the door with an easy gait. His week's pay would be folded into the back pocket of his overalls. He'd reach in, unfurl the bills, and with an air of pride and self-importance, dole out our allowance.

Then he'd take a long bath, put on his dress-up creased jeans and freshly laundered plaid shirt, splash on sweet-smelling cologne, and then, without fail, start yelling at us to find his shoes. "Where's my damn shoes?" We'd scurry around the house like rabbits looking for clover. It was always one shoe in one place, the other one hidden somewhere else. I swear he misplaced them on purpose. But once they were on his feet and he walked out the door, we knew any generous mood wasn't going to last. Storm clouds were bound to return.

Sure enough, a few hours later he would be back home

with his jeans and flannel shirt stale and stinking of alcohol and cigarettes. The emotional storm would build like a swirling tornado, and before long he would be crazed and violent, belittling and beating my mother. I didn't escape his wrath, either. He was over six feet tall and muscular from his work as a carpenter. You could sense his physical power even if he wasn't touching you. To me he looked like a terrifying giant. He'd stomp through the house in his heavy work boots, yelling about everything we were doing wrong. If anything got in his path, he would explode and his fists would fly. Almost in a supernatural way, his anger would turn his brown eyes into an electric green, and when that happened I knew the worst was still to come. This was our hell on earth, and Mamma and I were burning in its flames.

But no matter how bad it got, come Sunday morning my mother would lean over my bed, her fingers gently tapping my chest, and she'd be whispering, "Wake up, baby. Get ready. Let's go to church."

Our preacher happened to be my mother's uncle; we called him Uncle DJ. I'll admit that I wasn't always in the mood to hear him. But on one particular day the sermon he gave shook my soul to its core and watered the spiritual seed that had been growing inside me ever since that morning in Aunt Mae's kitchen when I learned you can talk to God.

"Children," our preacher bellowed from the pulpit. "God will answer your prayer. Just ask Him. He will answer. Yes, He will answer. No matter what you're going through, God will see you through it."

He screamed and spat those words out with a force that felt like it was delivered from celestial heights.

"Just ask Him!" the parishioners screamed and spat right back at him. "God will see you through it."

Truth is, there were plenty of times when I struggled in church to understand what was being said, but on this day, the message shot through me like an arrow that landed a bull's-eye in my heart. It didn't need to be explained. Jesus was in the house, and all you had to do was ask for help. I remember looking around and seeing several of the church sisters weeping and shouting, their arms raised and palms opened to the sky, swaying, rocking, jumping, some of them so filled with the Holy Ghost they almost lost their wigs.

I scanned the choir and fixed my eyes on Mamma. Tears were falling down her cheeks as she belted out the gospel. I assumed Mamma was still hurting from the night before. When the service was over and the choir broke up, I quickly made my way through the church and put my arms around her, trying my best to offer comfort. Pretty soon tears were falling from my eyes, too.

When we got to the car after the service, I asked why she was crying. She looked at me, her eyes still tearing up. "Because God is so good, baby. He will answer your prayer. Just ask Him."

I didn't have the courage to ask, "If I pray will he change my daddy?" I kept that question to myself and didn't utter a word. Even at a very young age I knew when to speak and when to stay silent.

But I couldn't get the preacher's words out of my head: "If you pray, God will see you through it. He'll answer your prayers."

That night, alone in my bedroom, I decided to put our preacher's claim to the test. While the moonlight was casting shadows on the wall and the evening cicadas were serenading, I got on my knees, clasped my hands together, leaned my elbows on the bed, and closed my eyes.

"God, I need you to answer my prayer. Please send me some little people to take care of and love," I whispered. "Let the people who are living inside our TV step out and talk to me and love me. I can love them back . . . I promise."

As an adult my prayer seems wildly fantastic, but when I was a kid, I believed the television actors on shows like *Gilligan's Island* and *The Brady Bunch* were real, even if they were only four inches tall. I didn't have the nerve to go behind the set and tear it apart to find out. My father would have killed me; we were still making payments on our state-of-the-art color TV.

There was no separation between what I saw on the screen and what my little boy's heart yearned to love. They were both real. I placed my faith in God and waited for my prayer to be answered.

+ What does it mean: "God will see you through it"?

• When has faith let you down?

• Did you know there are scientific studies showing that prayer changes our brain for the better? Check this out: www.andrewnewberg.com/research/.

4

Hearing the Answer

O NLY A FEW days later, my prayer was answered. When I came home from school, my mother's eyes were especially bright and her smile wide. She had some exciting news to tell me. Our neighbor from across the street was moving and wasn't able to take her parakeets, Fifi and Pierre, along with her. The neighbor asked if I could care for them. My father said, "Hell, no," but my mother said, "Yes."

"I won that round," my mother said with unbridled joy in her voice.

The next afternoon when I came home from school, Fifi and Pierre were sitting on a perch in their elegant three-story cage, chirping and chattering their litany of words. I *knew* in my heart that God had answered my prayers. He had offered up little people to talk to and to care for and love, and in that moment I had no doubt that He had heard me. It wasn't faith because faith means believing in something without proof. I had the proof. My heart flew open with the richness of this new knowledge.

Another child might not have made the connection, but I was becoming sensitive to what for me is the voice of God in my life and soul. The seed planted at Aunt Mae's that Mamma was helping to nourish was now gloriously manifesting. It's all about the experience of finding God, understanding that God is always present, and acknowledging that those little whispers I was hearing didn't mean I was going crazy. I was actually tuning in to His voice.

One way you can hear God is through voice, but there are many other ways, too. As the New Testament says in John 16:13 (ESV),

> *When the Spirit of truth comes, He will guide you into all the truth.*

I know God is always here. I don't know how I would have gotten to higher if I hadn't been able to experience God through my soul and in truth.

From that time forward, I've been trying to keep God's voice ever present in my life. Fifi and Pierre were still caged, but my soul was set free to hear God's voice. When I paid attention and listened, I soared.

• What's the difference between having faith and "knowing"?

- How do you "hear" God?

- Consider Psalms 77:11–12 (NIV*): *I will remember the deeds of the Lord; yes, I will remember your miracles of long ago. I will consider all your works and meditate on all your mighty deeds.* Perhaps you would like to keep a prayer journal to remember God's deeds.

---

* New International Version

5

Standing

B ACK IN THE day, Carter G. Woodson High School was the very definition of dilapidated. Paint and plaster peeled off its walls, the floors were pitted and cracked, and the plumbing barely functioned. The curriculum wasn't much better. Teaching and learning didn't seem to be the priority. On one side, across the street, stood the projects; on the other side was a litter-strewn park where folks would just hang out.

The school was in spitting distance of the "shotgun" housing where I lived. These houses were so named because you could stand at the front door and shoot a bullet straight through from the living room to the bedroom, the kitchen, the back bedroom, and then the bathroom.

My walking to school had its own excitement. In a way it was like watching a movie. I'd pass drug addicts, dealers, pimps, prostitutes, and plenty of hardworking folks. People of all ages, sizes, and shapes were hanging out on corners or in front of shops, sitting on porches, looking out windows, or rushing by on their way to work. It seemed like almost everyone was smoking cigarettes and standing in a menthol fog. Enormous boom boxes were hoisted on shoulders, and old stereos with speakers were set up on porches. I might hear Gladys Knight and the Pips on one block and Marvin Gaye on the next. It was a perfect soundtrack for my movie.

There were mangy stray dogs roaming the streets, and angry, barking ones in yards tied to posts, waiting for food to be thrown in their direction. I could deal with the dogs. The really unnerving critters were the sneaker-sized rats and giant shiny-backed, brownish-red cockroaches scurrying along the gutters and feasting inside garbage cans. When you opened a lid, the insects poured out into the light by the thousands, just like in a horror film.

One morning, when I reached the busy intersection of Washington Avenue and LaSalle Street, I noticed a tall man wearing dark glasses and a brown suit. He just stood on the corner, not moving, as the traffic light changed from red to green. He was as still as a statue. He held a cane in one hand and a folded aluminum chair under his arm, and in his other hand he grasped a shopping bag. As I came closer I realized he was blind and asking for help to navigate the crossing.

"Will someone help me cross the street? Will someone help me cross? Will someone please help me cross the street?" he repeated.

People passed him by, too wrapped up in their private worlds to hear him or to volunteer even if they did.

"I'll help you cross," I offered.

"Well, thank you, son," he said in a way that seemed as if he'd been expecting me. "Will you lend me your shoulder?"

He hooked his cane over his forearm, and I leaned in closer to better guide his hand onto my shoulder. We were about the same height. In careful syncopation we made our way across the street. When we were safely on the other side he told me his name.

"I'm Mr. Butler."

"Where are you going, Mr. Butler?"

"To Woodson to sell these praline candies." He gave the bag a little shake.

"That's where I'm going, too!" I said. "We can walk together."

So began our almost daily routine. On those mornings I met up with Mr. Butler, we talked and walked to school together, his cane tapping along with our steps. When we reached school, he gracefully unfolded his chair in front of the fence and offered me a delicious sticky treat, and we said our warm goodbyes.

"See you later, Mr. Butler. Good luck!"

"Thank you, son."

One day, after school was dismissed, I headed over to say hello to Mr. Butler before going home. From a few feet away, I observed a kid give him a dollar bill but claim it was a five.

Mr. Butler seemed to trust the world. He handed over the change for five dollars to his teenage customer without hesitation, no questions asked.

But I couldn't hold back.

"Mr. Butler, he's scamming you."

"Thank you, son," is all he said in response. It was the end of the story.

Over the weeks the bond between Mr. Butler and me grew stronger. Despite his blindness, he was one of the first souls who truly saw me, on the inside. In his company there were no rough edges or criticism, just appreciation for me. Maybe because Mr. Butler couldn't see the outside world, his understanding and acceptance of human nature, the inner landscape, was profound. He offered no judgments.

When you're a thirteen-year-old boy living in a world that doesn't always have much respect for you, where your own father's intent is only to demean you, the kindness and soul connection of someone like Mr. Butler can be a healing balm. My admiration for Mr. Butler was great. He was sightless, eking out a living by selling the sugar-and-butter candies his wife made every single day, with extraordinary discipline and dignity.

On a spring morning when New Orleans irises were beginning to bloom and the air was fragrant with hope, I walked up to the intersection. As usual, there was Mr. Butler with his cane, candy-filled bag, and folding chair. But this time he wasn't asking for help crossing the street. He was just standing there, still as ever.

I approached him without saying a word.

"I know you're there, son," he said.

"Yes, sir, I am!" Even I could hear the surprise in my voice.

"I was listening for *you*," he said.

"You were?"

"Yes. Sometimes in life, son, when you pray and you've said and done all you can, then all you have to do is stand and wait, and listen. Just stand."

The atmosphere felt different for a second, but at the time I truly did not grasp the meaning of Mr. Butler's words. I figured he assumed I would show up, as I had many times before, and it felt good to be thought of as responsible. But his message clearly made an impression because I remember it vividly, as if it were spoken today.

Now that I have some life under my belt, I understand what Mr. Butler meant. His words sit within me stronger than ever. It's a reference to scripture:

> Wherefore take unto you the whole armour of God, that ye may be able to withstand in the evil day, and having done all, to stand,
> from Ephesians 6:13 (KJV*),

and

> But if we hope for what we do not yet have, we wait for it patiently,
> from Romans 8:25 (NIV).

This turned out to be one of my most powerful lessons in faith. "If we hope for what we do not yet have, we wait for

---

* King James Version

it patiently." Years later, Mr. Butler's words remain a continual reminder. After you've done everything you need to do and it seems as if the world isn't stepping up to meet you, what do you do?

Stand.

Listen.

Wait patiently.

Keep waiting.

And ask yourself, "Have I ever offered someone my shoulder?"

- Think about a time in your life when you chose to stand. Do you regret it or did you learn from it?

- Is there a "Mr. Butler" in your life?

- Consider 1 Corinthians 15:58 (NET Bible*): *So then, dear brothers and sisters, be firm. Do not be moved! Always be outstanding in the work of the Lord, knowing that your labor is not in vain in the Lord.*

---

*   New English Translation Bible

PART TWO

Nourishing the Roots

ALL MY LIFE I'VE SEEN God everywhere, in everything. I find Him in a tablespoon of sugar, hear Him in the whisper of the wind through the trees, see Him in the clouds, and tune in to the resonance of His voice. These undeniable experiences strengthen my spiritual roots, and allow me to learn from my mistakes, to grow with confidence, and to dream big dreams.

As it says in Romans 8:28 (KJV),

And we know that all things work together for good to them that love God, to them who are the called according to his purpose.

My soul-filled experiences have taught me to embrace disappointments, knowing deeper lessons will be revealed; they've shown me God's hand in closing some doors and opening others; they've helped me release my past to create a future of hope; they've given me the tools to offer forgiveness, and put me back on the path whenever I lose my way. Strong roots are the faith from which grows the undeniable understanding that everything in life, the good and the bad, is a God-given opportunity to stand in the light. Everything.

6

Honoring

M Y CONNECTION WITH nature, and with trees in particular, is powerful. I believe my tree analogy first formed when I was about thirteen. Around this time, I started going to Greater Saint Stephen Full Gospel Baptist Church, where there was a tree painted in gold leaf on the lobby wall. The towering golden tree was divided into three sections: the roots at the bottom, the trunk midway, and branches spreading wide on top. The names of church members hung on each of the branches. I was so captivated by the deeper significance of the golden tree that every Sunday I'd spend lots of time just looking up at it.

Now I envision a tree whenever I'm thinking about the different souls who come into my life. Be it friends, family, mentors, employees, acquaintances, whoever—they are all subjected to my "Tree of Life" test.

First there are Leaf People. These are the folks who are in my life only for a season. I can't depend on them or count on them because they have weaknesses of their own and are only able to offer shade. Like leaves, they take what they need and as soon as it gets cold, or a fierce wind blows, or the rain comes, they're gone. I am not angry with them; it's just who they are.

Next there are Branch People. They are stronger than the Leaf People, but they need care. They may stick around from one season to the next, but if a storm rolls through, it's possible they'll break apart and I'll lose them. I know I have to test their strength before I can rely on them. It really depends on how long they've been growing with me. If it's been a while, they've probably gained strength with time. Newer branches may not be able to handle too much heaviness. They can split when the going gets tough. It's just who they are.

Then there are Root People. When I find someone who is like the roots of a tree, I know I've found someone special. Root People may be hard to find because they're not trying to be seen. They do their work underground. But quietly and without fanfare, they provide help and support and nourishment. They are happy when I thrive. Come what may, they support my soul. They hold my soul up. A tree may have many branches and many leaves, and only a few roots, yet it is the roots that are strong, resilient, and powerful.

My mother, of course, was a Root Person. I remember when I was around seven years old, I caught her staring with unbridled appreciation at a sleek racing-green Jaguar as it sped by.

"That's one beautiful car!" she exclaimed, eyes glittering as she took in its four-wheeled elegance.

"When I get big, Mamma, I'm going to buy you that car!" I said.

She turned and looked at me with a smile as bright as the stars. "Okay, baby," she said.

To be honest, I don't know if she believed it, but she sure made me feel that one day I would get her that car.

There were also plenty of times that Mamma was sad. Our home situation was brutal. Her husband was abusive, and we lived in poverty. She also suffered a number of serious medical conditions, from breast cancer to diabetes. But through it all Mamma remained resilient, like the roots of a mighty oak. Even as a child I felt a huge responsibility to try to make her feel better. I yearned to find the power to ease her pain.

"When I get big, I'm going to take care of you," I promised. "And you won't have to worry about a thing."

"Okay, baby," she would say. "I know you will."

I would go to my room and pray, "God, please bless me enough to take care of my mother." That's all I wanted in my young life. I didn't ask for toys or a trip to Disneyland. My wish was just to be able to take care of Mamma.

Years later, watching my mother come home from work worn and exhausted, burdened with her ill health, I knew what to say: "Mamma, I think it's time for you to retire."

She was quiet for a moment. "I'd like to do it, Junior, but I'm worried about making ends meet."

"I'll take care of you," I told her.

She was earning less than $500 a month, but to tell the truth, I was still worried about having enough money to pay the bills. My play *I Know I've Been Changed* was just starting to gain success. "What if it doesn't work out?" I wondered. But I didn't share my anxiety. Instead, I took a deep breath and repeated my words. "I made you a promise when I was a little boy," I said, looking deep into her eyes. "I *will* take care of you."

We both broke down and cried.

I am so grateful to my audience. God blessed me with them, and they are the reason why for the last twelve years my mother was on this earth she never had to worry about a roof over her head, bills, pills, or doctor's visits. The greatest gift I've ever been given is to be able to take care of my beautiful, amazing mamma—the strongest Root Person in my life.

And when it comes to Root People, this is what I've learned along the way: They are here to help you, but in turn, like the roots of any tree or plant, they need to be nourished, too. Water them with love, appreciation, gratitude, and generosity. They want the best for you, and if your heart is open, you'll want the best for them, too.

◆ Who are the Leaf, Branch, and Root People in your life?

◆ What are *you* in other people's lives?

• How do you react when leaves and branches let you down?

• How can you help to nourish the roots in your life?

7

Protecting Your Dreams

WHEN I WAS a kid I built a small fort under the porch of our house. It wasn't much more than a cramped cubbyhole painted robin's-egg blue, but it was my personal paradise. Even though I could still hear the thump of my father's footsteps through the floorboards overhead, his bitter and vile words to Mamma, and the terror of his raging storms, my fort offered the protection of another world. It was my shelter, my refuge. It was a place where my imagination could roam free. Here I could safely weave my daydreams for hours on end. It was my personal kid-safety zone where I could play and imagine without interruption.

Later on, I learned to be careful about sharing my dreams. I found out there are unfortunate souls who I came to think of as "dream killers" or "dream thieves." If I shared my dreams with these naysayers I would be met with:

"You can't do that."

Why not?

"Because you're poor."

"Because you're black."

"Because you're from the ghetto."

These people, and I'm sure you know a few, are infected with negativity or fear. If your dream brings light, if your dream brings hope, if your dream brings peace, if your dream is bigger than anything they could ever imagine, they will try to tear it down. They usually don't do it out of malice. They do it because your dreams feel as far away to them as the moon and stars. Your dreams make them feel small.

After years of ridicule, I learned to treat my dreams as if they were precious gems hidden in a velvet pouch. I kept these dream treasures tucked away in a safe place within my soul, out of reach of those who doubted me. Sadly, at times this included my mother. Mamma loved me to her core, but she also wanted to protect me. It wasn't her fault. She had grown up in the Jim Crow South when black people weren't allowed to dream big. The possibility of a person of color having any kind of success, other than working at the phone company and getting benefits, was something she couldn't imagine. My dream was too big for her to understand because it meant reaching higher and taking chances.

When I was twenty years old and putting on my first play in Birmingham, Alabama, I had to use my mother's credit card to rent a van to get there. The bill was around three hundred dollars. But the show didn't make any money, and when I came home I had to tell her I couldn't pay for the rental.

Mamma was furious. "You never gonna make it, Junior," she said. "You need to stop thinking about those plays. Just go get yourself a job with the phone company. Get those benefits."

"That's not my life," I told her. "I have dreams. I have more than *that* inside me."

"Well, you're never going to make it," she said, turning herself around in the chair and taking a deep drag on her cigarette. I watched the smoke rise like a chimney.

When Mamma finally turned back around to face me, she saw tears pouring from my eyes, and when she did, blood drained from her face. She saw how her words had broken me. She apologized right away.

Still my heart ached, and I couldn't help but question my dream. When I prayed for guidance and heard God's answer, I could release Mamma's reaction. How could she see the world any differently? I knew Momma wasn't trying to be mean; she was just trying to protect me. When people have never felt the power of their own wings, they can't imagine taking flight.

Being angry with dream killers or feeling sorry for them doesn't help. You might find, as I did, that the people you love the most are the ones most capable of infecting your dreams with doubt and negativity.

So what's the answer?

Conjure compassion instead of resentment. Matthew 7:12 (ESV) says,

> So whatever you wish that others would do to you, do also to them, for this is the Law and the Prophets.

It doesn't mean you stop loving naysayers. Love them even more because they need it. What's more, you need some naysayers in your life. You need people to challenge your point of view. Your job is to look for the truth in their negativity. For instance, sometimes I'll get a bad review, and my first defensive reaction is to think it's completely off the mark. Once I give myself a moment and allow my initial reaction to be released, I'll read it again to see if there's anything I can learn from the review. If it's pure vitriol, well, I let it go. But if there's some truth, even a kernel, I'll use what's written to be better at what I do. I can take constructive criticism.

You have these kinds of choices, too. Keep your vision to yourself. Or, like me, know you can also use negative words to spur you on and make you work even harder to prove the naysayers wrong.

Let me suggest something more: Be modest and patient; allow your dream its own time to grow. Dreams need to be tended like crops before you can enjoy the harvest.

And this is important: Don't get hung up on the outcome. Hand that over to God. Remember, He's the one at the wheel. Of course, I was afraid of failing, but I held on to my faith, worked toward my dream, and then surrendered.

Also, encourage yourself. If someone puts your dream down, that's when it's time to encourage yourself. When I wanted to live in a big house and it was still only a fantasy, I'd visit open houses. I'd test-drive cars I wanted to own. I'd sit outside restaurants and watch happy families eating together. These were ways I encouraged myself to know that whatever dreams I had, they were already out there in the world waiting for me. It was a reminder that everything I dreamt about was possible.

Nurture your imagination with hard work, positive energy, ease, and self-encouragement. Cherish your dreams and keep them safe. When others try to tear you down, raise yourself up by knowing God is in your secret fort; he's in your house.

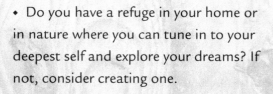

• Do you have a refuge in your home or in nature where you can tune in to your deepest self and explore your dreams? If not, consider creating one.

• Be honest with yourself: Are *you* the dream killer? What do you tell yourself about your dreams?

• Have you asked God for help in realizing your dreams?

• Consider Proverbs 19:21 (ESV): *Many are the plans in the mind of a man, but it is the purpose of the Lord that will stand.*

8

Releasing the Past

THERE'S NO MAGIC time machine to reset the clock or reinvent our childhoods, but we can alter the present and future by changing how we think and feel about what's happened in our past. No matter how difficult or disturbing your memories, they don't have to crush your soul. You can transcend your experience. You can change your reaction. You can forgive.

My father, Emmitt, was a functional alcoholic and an abuser. He brutalized us. If you look at photographs of me as a child, you'll see me smiling. But look closely into my eyes, and you'll see the pain and terror in them. Inside I was crying for help, for release from the agony. By the time I reached adolescence, the fear and misery had turned to smoldering anger.

But I didn't leave home right away. I was twenty-one before I could make it out; I needed to know there was really a world of possibilities outside New Orleans. That world opened up to me on my first visit to Atlanta during "Freaknik," a sort of spring break without the beach for black college kids. I wasn't in college, but I went anyway. While all the kids were getting numbed out, drinking and partying, I was waking up to possibility. For the first time in my life, I saw there were black people doing great things with their lives. There were black doctors, lawyers, business owners, and well-off families going to restaurants, the theater, and movies. I knew Atlanta was the place for me.

As soon as I got back home to New Orleans, I told Mamma, "I'm moving to Atlanta."

I could tell she was sad, but as usual she put me first. "If you ever need to come home, Junior," she said, "I'll always be here for you." We hugged, but I knew, I just knew, I would never go back to a house where Emmitt was living. I packed, and closed the door on Baronne Street.

My first several years in Atlanta turned out to be a life-and-death struggle. I managed to get through the spring, summer, and autumn living paycheck to paycheck, but during the chilly months of winter, the money ran out and I couldn't pay my rent. The unthinkable happened. I became homeless. I'd sleep in my car and try to keep warm by running the heater or wrapping myself in a quilt Aunt Mae had given me. If I had some cash, I'd crash in a pay-by-the-week hotel room.

The hotel had a heavyweight atmosphere of hopelessness; most folks walked around slowly, without energy or any real light in their eyes, either addicted to drugs or just down on their luck. The air was thick with misery—and toxic fumes.

There was only a gap of a few feet from my room's door to the parked cars on the street. Early in the mornings, people would gun their engines to warm their cars. Puffs of exhaust blew into my room like filthy gray clouds. I usually got out of bed, walked outside, and asked the drivers to please turn their cars to face a different direction.

But one cold morning, I'd given up. Lost my hope. Lost my faith. Lost my dreams. I was in such despair I really didn't want to live anymore. I smelled the exhaust and saw it pouring into my room and didn't care. "Let the poison fill my lungs. Take me to the other side," I prayed. "Release me from this dream-killing life."

Well, you know that didn't work. The fumes didn't kill me, and God brought me back to faith and release. Feelings of hopelessness were there for a reason. That very day I finally had the strength to let Emmitt have it. It probably helped that we were speaking on the phone, and he wasn't intimidating me with his physical presence.

"You're a horrible person," I screamed into the receiver. "How could you have treated me so bad?"

It didn't take him any time at all to answer. "You don't know what happened to me" was all he said before he hung up.

Then . . . silence.

It was one of those moments of surprising grace. There was a space that opened in my soul, and forgiveness took up temporary residency. When I put the phone's receiver back on its cradle, I felt something in me lift. The darkness didn't dissolve right away, but something was dislodged. I felt it.

Healing with compassion and forgiveness, I've learned, can come in other surprising ways. In 2013, a producer from *CBS This Morning* contacted me and asked if I would consider writing a letter to my younger self. It was never anything I'd thought of doing, but the idea struck a chord within me.

On a flight from Los Angeles to New York, I wrote the letter to my thirteen-year-old self. Flying is one of the few opportunities I get to disconnect from constant demands and interruptions. On this morning, I rolled down the shade, opened my laptop, and let my memories and heart open like the golden horizon. This is what I wrote:

> I know you don't know this right now, but who you become is being shaped inside every one of the experiences you're having. The good, the bad, and yes, even the ugly ones. . . .
>
> I know there's also a part of you that worries that you won't live to be thirty years old. I want you to know now that you will, and it's going to be okay. When you think you have no one to protect you, you have something inside protecting you. When you are told you are nothing, and something inside says, "Don't believe that," that is the voice of God. When a teacher tells you that you'll never be successful because you are poor and black, and something inside you says, "She's wrong. That's not true," that is also the voice of God.
>
> I know the most important thing right now for you is that you want to grow up and do well enough to be able to take care of your mother. I know you're worried about her. I know you're very concerned. You're thirteen right now, and you're worried she won't live to see your fourteenth birthday. So you aim to take on a great burden and you

*want to do all you can. I want you to know that it's going
to be okay. You're going to take care of her. And she lives
for thirty more years. She sees you thrive and be happy,
and more than anything, you see her living the best life she
ever could. That's because of you. You make her proud.*

Meanwhile, the plane sailed through the clouds. As it
began its descent hours later into the wintry city, I looked at
the ice blue skyline coming into view and suddenly felt another great weight lifted from my chest. Another boulder
of anger I had been carrying around was released, and I felt
an overwhelming sense of lightness, an airy, buoyant sensa-
tion.

Rereading the letter now, I can see I wanted to offer my
angry adolescent self a sanctuary from the hell he was
going through. I wanted him to know that the horrors he
was experiencing were not all there would be of his life. I
wanted to talk to him about trusting in God's voice, having
faith, and allowing his soul to help him when he felt his
heart harden and break apart. I wanted him to know that
one day his heart would soften with understanding and forgiveness. Most important, I wanted him to lay his worry
aside. I wanted him to know he would be there for his
mamma. He would live to take care of her when she needed
him most.

It's true you can't turn back time and you can't change
your history, but a letter to your younger self can turn
memory's kaleidoscope and switch the image. Instead of
viewing your childhood with sadness or anger, you can
offer that child tenderness and hope. Turn the kaleidoscope

again and find gratitude for the trials you survived and the strength and wisdom they brought you.

Turn it again and see that God's grace is sometimes fierce, but He's always present.

• Write a letter to your thirteen-year-old self. What will you caution yourself about? What will you tell yourself to look forward to?

9

———————

Feeling Worthy

E VEN THOUGH I had three siblings—a younger
brother, Emmbre, and two older sisters, Melva and
Yulanda—more often than not, it felt as if I were my mother's only child. My fondest memories of times together
were our Sunday mornings in church—just the two of us.
When we were in God's sanctuary, we could safely open
our hearts and let our souls be free and vulnerable. Church
was our refuge, and Jesus, as my mother taught me, was
our rock.

We shared laughter, joy, and faith, but at home we suffered unimaginable abuse at the hands of her husband—the
man I called father. We managed to hold on because of our
love for each other and our faith in God. I knew she loved
me every single minute of my life. I knew Mamma loved
me with every fiber of her soul. I knew she loved me uncon-
ditionally. The power of her love allowed me to have hope.

That said, my mother, Maxine, was also a closed woman,
a private soul. Getting personal information out of her
wasn't as easy as turning a tap and watching the water pour

out of a faucet. It had to be the right time, when she was feeling relaxed and unburdened. Sometimes, on those rare occasions, the spout would open and information trickled out. Here's what I gleaned over the years:

Maxine's mother died when Maxine was thirteen years old, leaving her father to raise five children alone in the rural town of Amite City, Louisiana. It was a struggle, but love was always present, and it helped them stay close and get by.

At sixteen, Maxine met a young man named Emmitt. He was about nineteen or twenty, but his real age was not known because he didn't have a birth certificate. What Emmitt did have was a serious case of swagger. Tall and well built, he rode into Amite City high and mighty in a big shiny new car, his strong arm slung over the passenger seat as if he was just waiting for it to be filled. On each visit in the weeks that followed he'd be sitting behind the wheel of a different swanky car—a gleaming Cadillac one week, the next a Buick. The teenaged Maxine couldn't help but be impressed by this handsome, flashy stranger. She was dazzled.

Emmitt oozed confidence. He boasted that he was rich, said he had a huge cattle ranch in Texas. He bragged that all those brand-new cars were his. He wove his stories with such bravado and confidence that my young, impressionable mother didn't have a chance. He won her over in no time at all. After just a short period of dating, Emmitt asked her to marry him. Without skipping a beat, Maxine went straight to her father with her handsome suitor's request.

"This man is rich, Daddy, and he wants to marry me," she told him, pleading for his approval.

My savvy grandfather, who owned a juke joint, always carried a straight razor in his pocket, and was nobody's fool, saw the truth behind Emmitt's big-man act. He knew he was a fake.

"That [expletive] is lying to you!" he warned my mother. "He's a nickel slick and a dollar short."

But my mother was insistent. She wore her father down until, finally, he gave his consent.

Once he agreed, my grandfather took Emmitt aside and said, "You take a good look at my daughter. Check her out from head to toe. She don't have a scar on her nowhere. If ever you don't want her, you bring her back to me the same way you found her."

My mother was just seventeen when she married, and in most ways still a child, filled with fairy-tale ideas about romance. After the wedding ceremony, Maxine waved goodbye to Amite City and climbed into Emmitt's Cadillac. They drove right down to New Orleans, a place Mamma called "the big city," and pulled up to a juke joint called Cooks. My mother thought they were there to get a couple of drinks at the bar to celebrate the marriage. She figured it wouldn't be long before they got back in the car and embarked on their honeymoon.

But hours went by and her new husband didn't make a move. Finally she said, "Come on, honey, let's go to the ranch."

Emmitt spat back, "Girl, I wasn't doing nothing but lying

to you. I ain't got no damn ranch. That ain't even my car. I just test-drive them on the weekends." He laughed ruefully. "I'm sitting here trying to find someone who'll give us a place to stay."

That was the end of my mother's so-called honeymoon and the beginning of her lifetime of hell.

In the earliest days of their marriage, Emmitt began to beat her . . . and beat her . . . and beat her. When she went to her aunts asking for help and advice, one of them told her, "He's a good man. He's got a good job. Stay with him."

And so she did.

At eighteen years old, she found herself pregnant with my sister, and at nineteen pregnant again with my other sister. The abuse, beating, yelling, and belittling never stopped. At twenty-four years, she was pregnant again, and there I was, born into it.

As a child, I would watch them fight and see this man doing horrific things to my mother. A child has an uncanny ability to take on the responsibility of every problem that is going on with a parent they love. They take on the burden. I was no exception. Every chance I got, I tried to ease my mother's pain by making her laugh or at least smile. At five years old, I held her tight, sitting snug under her arm, offering comfort after my father had beaten her. Even at that young age, I wondered why she stayed with him.

I remember one really horrible fight when he was tearing into my mother—and then he came after me with a fury I had never seen before. I was beaten bloody that night.

"Look at what he's done, Mamma," I cried. I thought to myself that we would surely leave him now. But the next day, Emmitt apologized. We didn't leave. And again, I was left wondering, *Why does she stay?*

One night I told my mother something that I had kept a secret. I had seen Emmitt touching one of my sister's young girlfriends inappropriately. When I told my mother, the look of panic and shock in her eyes made me feel like I might have shattered her soul. My own heart split open.

She gathered my sisters together and asked if Emmitt had ever touched them. They both emphatically said no. Everyone was in tears, and I thought, "Oh, God, why did I say anything? This is all my fault."

Then my mother marched into the living room, where Emmitt was sitting in his chair, drinking a beer. She confronted him about the friend. They got into a screaming fight. But this time Mamma did something she never did before. She grabbed her children and put us in the car. Just as we were about to drive away, Emmitt stormed out of the house, his face contorted in rage. He reached inside the passenger window, grabbed my arm and squeezed it, hard. He snarled, "You tell her *this*? You little [expletive], I'll tell you something. . . . I'll get you."

My mother gunned the gas, and we drove off.

That night we stayed in one of my aunts' houses and I remember how good it felt, so quiet and safe. But it didn't last. About three in the morning, I woke to the sound of Emmitt's voice in the next room begging my mother for forgiveness. The next thing I know, the light was flicked on in our room, and my mother was standing over the bed.

"Get your things, children," she said. "We're going home."

"What? We're going back?" I asked in disbelief. "Why?"

She didn't answer me, just grabbed our stuff and hurried us out the door.

Decades later, I look back on my mother's decisions, not through the lens of a child, but as a man who still loves her without judgment. I look back as a man with a family of his own, and as a man who has made his own share of mistakes. My life experience has helped me to understand why my mother stayed.

I know now that when a child is growing up, abusive voices echo loudly. I can still hear the damning things Emmitt said to me. Because of his cruelty, for many years, I didn't feel as if I deserved to be happy or successful. I didn't feel worthy because I had his voice resonating in my head, telling me that I was nothing, that I was horrible, that I didn't deserve anything good in life. When you grow up being told those things every day, they take root in your subconscious and undermine every positive event in your life.

I was able to work through my toxic childhood, but my mother never had that chance. She was only a child when she married her abuser, and, unfortunately, she believed his words. Mamma also grew up in the South, with daily humiliations like being forced to sit in the back of the bus and drink from a separate water fountain. How could she feel worthy, having to follow these laws that inflicted shame and degradation?

Our work is to help one another get to the place where we understand that we are all worthy, despite our histories.

You are worthy because God gave you breath in your body.

You have a right to walk this planet just like everyone else.

You have a right to every good and perfect gift, because God said you are good and perfect.

I challenge you to get to worthy.

You might be thinking, "But you don't know the shameful things I did in my past."

I get it, but I'm still saying, "You are worthy."

When you know your worth, when you know your value, your life changes and you change lives.

Whatever you do, get to worthy. Once you're there, help someone else get there, too.

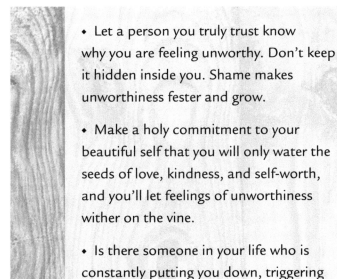

• Let a person you truly trust know why you are feeling unworthy. Don't keep it hidden inside you. Shame makes unworthiness fester and grow.

• Make a holy commitment to your beautiful self that you will only water the seeds of love, kindness, and self-worth, and you'll let feelings of unworthiness wither on the vine.

• Is there someone in your life who is constantly putting you down, triggering

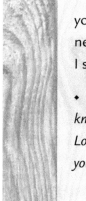

your feelings of inadequacy? You don't need this person. Ask yourself, "Why am I staying?"

• Consider Jeremiah 29:11 (ESV): *For I know the plans I have for you, declares the Lord, plans for welfare and not for evil, to give you a future and a hope.*

10

Filling the House

I N THIS ERA of instant gratification and gotta-have-it-now impatience, it's hard to imagine putting everything you have, and I mean *everything*—all your money, all your energy, all your hopes—into a dream, then meeting the hard knocks of failure over and over again, falling down and getting up . . . having to push yourself up to rise and try again for seven long years.

The first time I put on my play *I Know I've Been Changed,* I took for granted that it would be a huge success. I envisioned folks lining up outside the theater and filling all the seats. I could hear their loud laughter and endless applause resounding in my ears. Feeling optimistic, in the summer of 1993 I spent every cent from my income tax return, money that should have gone to a car payment and money that should have gone to my apartment, and rented the 14th Street Playhouse in downtown Atlanta. I hired actors, built scenery, and rented props. I did the whole nine yards on my own, spending all I had to my name.

The theater had seating for two hundred people. You

know how many seats were filled on opening night? Thirty. That's right. Thirty. When I looked out and saw all that emptiness, my heart sank to the bottom. I was so naïve, assuming people would just show up. On top of that, I'd booked the theater for Fourth of July weekend. I had a lot to learn. For one thing, who goes to a play on the Fourth of July? People are barbecuing and watching fireworks. Also, I was a total unknown. No one had heard of Tyler Perry, no one knew about my play. Why would they come?

Did it stop me? No. The next time I put on the show, I did it in New Orleans. This time I tried to promote it by putting up flyers and sending out press releases and spreading the word, but it didn't work. Hardly anyone showed up. The theater was less than half full.

Did it stop me? No. I was determined to make it happen. I felt strongly this was what I was supposed to do; this was my path. My destiny. I was going to show all those people who didn't believe in me that they were dead wrong.

Every year for five years I spent every cent I had on *I Know I've Been Changed,* putting it on in different cities and in different theaters. Every single show—every one—failed. The financial failure and the heartbreak tore at my faith. Yet something kept the dream alive in my mind and in my heart and so I kept going, kept hoping, until finally, in 1998, I'd had it. I wanted to give up. I was ready to do what Mamma told me to do: give up my pie-in-the-sky aspirations and work at the phone company and start collecting those benefits.

I was on my way to the phone company to apply for a job when some guys I knew who were sort of in show business approached me to do the play one more time at Atlanta's historic House of Blues, where such acts as the Blues Brothers, James Cotton, Luther "Guitar Jr." Johnson, and Booker T and the M.G.'s had appeared.

I agreed to do it, but the night the show was opening, March 12, 1998, was the coldest night I'd ever felt in Atlanta. And the heat was out in the theater. I was sitting in the dressing room, angry, frustrated, and feeling empty and hopeless. I was so agitated with disappointment that I couldn't sit still. I stood up and started pacing back and forth and speaking out loud to God. "You bring me out to these moments and you never see me through. What's going on?"

After that outcry, all emotion was drained from me. I sat down defeated and started applying the makeup to play Old Man Joe, a character I created long before Madea. Suddenly, I heard God's voice, the one I've heard ever since I was a kid. "I tell you when it's over. You don't tell me when it's over. Now get up again and look out the window."

I moved to the window—and saw a miracle. People were lined up around the corner, waiting to get into the theater. They were bundled up in coats, blowing into their hands, shivering, standing in the frigid air to see my play. Tears came to my eyes. "God," I asked, "what is this?" Silence was my answer. Success was happening.

A couple of weeks later, the play was produced at the Fox Theatre, with more than 4,500 seats, and it sold out—two shows. Every national promoter I had spoken with during the past seven years, every one who had turned me down, now had offers in hand to take me on tour. Before long I was playing arenas with 20,000 seats and filling every one of them.

As I look back over the long, hard road that took me from disappointment to success, I realize there were two forces driving me. One was the overwhelming desire to be able to take care of my mother. The other? To be honest, it was rage. I carried fury and anger like a fiery ball in my gut. "I'll show you, Emmitt. I'll show you." This thought propelled me to keep going.

But it didn't give me any peace or satisfaction. Even though the theaters were packed, the audiences applauding and standing on their feet, I was still scared it wouldn't last. That's because when you're driven by anger, rage, and revenge, you can't relax into it. You can't appreciate success. You're not tuned in to the happiness life offers. You're on edge all the time.

My life didn't feel safe. Despite the play's success, I didn't hold a deep sense of comfort or joy. It was only when, years later, I was able to forgive Emmitt, that the fuel firing me was no longer anger but love and compassion. That's when my life really turned around.

Once that happened, I met true success.

• Anger is a human emotion and it's not always negative. But it's not good to hold on to it for long. A study by the

University of Georgia showed that moderate exercise like running, riding a bike, or walking fast after an upsetting event can help you release your anger.

• Recall a time when you could turn your anger into forgiveness.

11

Taking One Step at a Time

A FEW YEARS AGO, I got into the habit of running five miles every day. It took me around an hour to meet my goal. Real runners out there know I wasn't breaking any records, but I'm a large man, so I chose a reasonable pace that left me exhilarated, not too exhausted, and with enough energy for a full day of work.

Early in the morning, I'd put on my running uniform: loose, lightweight shorts, a long T-shirt, running shoes, and a sports watch that recorded my distance and time. I'd also wear a hat as low as I could over my forehead and a pair of sunglasses. Satisfied I was dressed for comfort and anonymity, I'd head for Atlanta's Silver Comet Trail, where nature's bounties are on unabashed display.

At one time the trail was a railroad track linking Smyrna, Georgia, to central Alabama. When the railroad was no longer used, the track was abandoned until visionaries turned it into a beloved trail for runners, hikers, and bike riders. On my run I'd pass tall trees whose branches created a leafy arc overhead, plenty of Georgia pines letting off their Christmas tree aroma, a wooden covered bridge, open terrain with views of lush fields, old farmhouses, and awe-inspiring rock formations. You might say I was jogging through paradise. Running opened the door to my senses, and I was able to take it all in. I felt my breath moving like a miracle through my body. I'd be clearheaded, in tune with nature, grateful, close to God.

I listened to inspiring, positive tunes. Tim McGraw or Faith Hill, Tupac, Stevie Wonder, Sounds of Blackness—any upbeat music kept me moving ahead. Truthfully, I needed all the help I could get, because my people are from New Orleans. In other words, our philosophy is *laissez les bons temps rouler*—let the good times roll. Or to put it another way—eat, die, and eat some more. I was particularly proud of my running routine since I was once again bucking my upbringing; I was taking care of myself. Running was a total win-win.

And then . . .

. I stopped running.

Why do we stop doing the very things that nurture us physically and emotionally, and feed our spiritual growth? It's a big question, one always worth contemplating. At this particular time, I stopped running because I was drawn so fully into my work that my focus narrowed and I shut out some of the things that truly mattered most. The desire to achieve in my career became all-consuming, and for a while, I lost my sense of balance. I offer this not as an excuse, but as an observation.

Eventually, when my broader awareness reawakened (and after seriously scrutinizing myself in a full-length mirror), I remembered the strength, clarity, and happiness that running gave me. After a few months of slacking off and feeling the ill effects, I decided to make an effort to get back on track.

The bad news?

I learned that once you take a break, it's not so easy to get back in the groove again.

Every day I'd put on my sneakers, shorts, and T-shirt, wrap my sports watch around my wrist, pull my cap down over my forehead, slip on my sunglasses, and make what I thought was an easy deal with myself: "Just one nonstop mile today."

No go.

I couldn't reach even *that* goal. I'd start out at a fast clip and then exhaustion would stop me cold—or, rather, in a sweaty heap. When I checked the distance on my watch and saw I hadn't even run close to a mile, frustration would spread through my veins like a stain. I felt hopeless. All the energy and enthusiasm drained out of me.

"I'm too tired to go on," I'd tell myself, shrug my shoulders, and walk back to my car, feeling defeated and annoyed with myself.

One day, after yet another failed running attempt, I confessed to a good friend how frustrated I was about my sorry running chops. "Tyler, you've got it all wrong," he said. "It's not about the speed or the distance. It's about the endurance."

I rolled his words around my mind and remembered Ecclesiastes 9:11 (KJV):

I returned, and saw under the sun, that the race is not to the swift, nor the battle to the strong, neither yet bread to the wise, nor yet riches to men of understanding, nor yet favour to men of skill; but time and chance happeneth to them all.

The next day I resumed my running and consciously chose endurance over speed. I decided not to check my watch to see how far I had gone or how long it was taking me until I had reached the end of my run. I focused instead on what was right in front of me, one step at time. I paid attention to the beauty of the world around me, the air I was breathing. I thanked God for where I was, fully alive and in the moment.

Before I knew it, I had run two miles. *Two miles!* I thanked God for those two miles. It wasn't five, but it was a beginning—and it was perfect.

While I celebrated with my hands waving in the air, I thought about the power of staying in the race no matter what obstacles are present. It made me think about how we can set a huge goal for ourselves, one that may be really tough to reach. It can seem hopeless or even impossible. Circumstances in our lives may distract us. We may forget to stop along the way to take note of our small victories. Instead of staying in the present, appreciating the gifts of the here and now, we get lost in the future. We can get frustrated because we think we're running out of time. We may forget to say, "Thank you, God, for where I am right now."

If that happens, you need to know this: Even though you haven't reached your goal yet, with each step you are getting closer. Don't think about the finish line. Enjoy the race! Don't allow yourself to become overwhelmed with how far you still have to go.

Focus on one step at a time.

Be grateful for how far you've come.

Thank God for where you are.

Keep going.

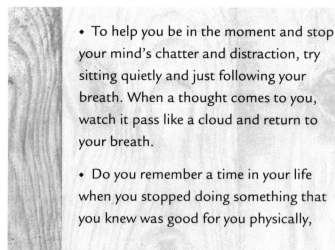

• To help you be in the moment and stop your mind's chatter and distraction, try sitting quietly and just following your breath. When a thought comes to you, watch it pass like a cloud and return to your breath.

• Do you remember a time in your life when you stopped doing something that you knew was good for you physically,

spiritually, or emotionally? It's never too late to begin again.

• Do you have a daily exercise routine? It doesn't have to be Olympic-style. If you're able, even a ten-minute walk is better than nothing.

12

Learning in Reverse

A S MY LIFE continues to unfold with God's grace, the instruction gets clearer every day: Your beginning doesn't have to dictate your destination. You can learn in reverse.

Emmitt's cruel actions, his impatience, disrespect, uncontrollable anger, and violence, taught me all the ways I *didn't* want to be like him. My father stomped through our house, shooting his ugly, bone-chilling stare in my direction and sneering, "There's that little son of a bitch. Look at that jackass."

Can you imagine how those words stung a young, innocent soul? I'll never forget his tyranny, but it is because of his behavior that I consciously choose to model wholly different behaviors. I'm grateful that I gained the ability to take lessons from my past and turn them around to create a light-guided present.

In direct opposition to how my father raised me, with my own son I focus on being a parent who is tender and loving, attentive, curious, supportive, patient, and aware.

I'm not a perfect soul, but I strive to keep my heart open and loving. I've sworn never to utter an unkind word to my son, Aman. You might think, "Oh, that's just common sense." Perhaps, but it's different for people like myself who have been raised in a hostile, violent environment. We have to turn our damaging early role models upside down, inside out, and all around. We have to be vigilant not to perpetuate the damages we ourselves suffered. Emmitt said he was beaten as a child, but he didn't recognize it as abuse. We know that these behaviors get passed down, generation to generation.

It takes awareness and consciousness to stop these cycles. One day I was walking through the house with Aman, and I was in a hurry to pick something up in the next room. But on our way, my son got totally captivated by what was right in front of him. With typical toddler focus and fascination, he stopped in his tracks, pointed, and cried out with utter joy, "Papa, look! Piano! Piano!"

I was in a hurry, but I made a conscious decision not to rush him and to respond to his enthusiasm. I followed his cue, pulled out the bench, helped him climb up, and gently placed his little fingers on the keys.

My father never would have set his clock to my desires, and he would have broken my fingers before he let me sit at a piano. He would have thought, "That's not what boys do. That's not what men do." It was almost as if my father's purpose in life was to kill a child's dream rather than nurture it. He couldn't stand to see me, or really anyone, take pleasure in life.

My intention is to support my son's dreams, encourage

him to explore whatever captivates him, and join in his wonder. That's what I mean by consciously embracing another way of being than the one that may have been imprinted in us through our own experience.

Here's another example of learning in reverse. Soccer is part of my two-year-old's soul. He probably gets his enthusiasm and athletic gifts from his mother, who used to play soccer in Ethiopia and still enjoys playing. Every chance we get, Aman and I are outside on the lawn running and kicking the ball around. When I was young, my father did everything he could to thwart me from exploring my interests and actively sought to damage whatever self-esteem I had. I want to allow Aman's life to unfurl freely like the petals on a flower.

Which reminds me . . . Aman and I were walking through the garden one day, and he said, "I want to bring Mommy a rose."

Without hesitation, I clipped the rose, made sure there were no sharp thorns, and handed it to him. He put the flower up to his nose and inhaled deeply.

"Mmmmmm," he said, a big smile spreading across his apple cheeks. "Smell it," he directed, lifting the flower up to my nose.

I have to admit, at the time I was thinking about all the things I had to do and was feeling overwhelmed by the work ahead of me, but in an instant my little boy once again brought me into the here and now.

"Smell this flower," he insisted.

I sniffed the rose's sweet scent.

Watching me closely with his saucer-sized eyes, he said, "Mmmm . . . good!"

And it was.

Aman led me to a place of peace, presence, and true purpose. I was a child imprisoned by fear, but my son is free to enjoy his days and share his pleasure.

My prayer is that Aman will always be in touch with this sense of wonder, his appreciation for the beauty of the natural world, and that when he looks back on his magical, loving childhood, he will want to pay it forward.

• What kind of relationship did you have with your parents? Do you express gratitude for lessons learned, good or bad?

• How might you pay it forward?

• Consider Ezekiel 18:20 (ESV): *The son shall not suffer for the iniquity of the father, nor the father suffer for the iniquity of the son. The righteousness of the righteous shall be upon himself, and the wickedness of the wicked shall be upon himself.*

13

Discovering the Gift

EVERYONE WHO KNOWS me understands it's practi-
cally impossible to buy me a gift. It's not because I'm
choosy or critical. It's more that I'm so profoundly fortu-
nate in my life I probably already own all, or maybe most,
of the cool stuff out there that I am interested in. That's
why I tell friends and family who want to give me a present
to please handwrite me a letter instead. It's rarely done
these days, and I cherish this kind of personal attention and
effort. I've kept every single such handwritten letter I've
ever received.

About two years ago someone I care a great deal about
gave me a gift that wasn't a letter. I thanked her for it and
put the box in the trunk of my car with every intention of
opening it once I arrived home. But once I got there, I got
busy. And, I'm embarrassed to admit, I forgot about the gift
for quite a while, maybe months. The box had fallen in a bin
in the trunk, hidden from view. I guess it was a case of out
of sight, out of mind—but no excuses!

One day while looking for something else I'd misplaced,

I discovered the gift—a gift I'd forgotten I even had. After I opened it, I immediately phoned the gift giver and thanked her for the thoughtful present. It turned out to be the perfect gift. I also apologized from the bottom of my heart for not calling sooner. Frankly, I was a little embarrassed.

"You *that* damn busy?" she chided.

We shared a good laugh.

The present was a sports watch with all the bells and whistles, including a fitness tracker, heart rate sensor, built-in GPS, music player, and lots more. It was very cool and I knew I would use it on my morning runs.

Even better, it brought my mind and soul to this reflective place: This gift, which turns out to be so useful, has been with me all this time, but I left it tucked away, hidden and ignored. Everywhere I drove, I took it with me and didn't even know I had it. There were days when I could have used this gift to make my life better—but I didn't know it was within reach.

With this thought resonating, I realized that we all have gifts within, but they're too often hidden. We have gifts we have never used, even though they are within reach. If we only knew where to look, we would find them. These gifts are special. They might even change our lives and help make the world a better place.

We all have gifts given to us by God.

Look for yours.

• As you travel through life, why not commit to searching your soul for all your hidden gifts?

• How can you use the gifts God has given you to help spread hope, love, and joy in our world?

• Consider 1 Peter 4:10 (ESV): *As each has received a gift, use it to serve one another, as good stewards of God's varied grace.*

14

Planting What You
Want to Grow

I MAGINE YOU GO to a nursery and buy the seeds of a fruit tree. You get home, choose the perfect spot in your yard, dig a hole just the right size, and gingerly place the seeds inside it. Gently you put the earth back on top, covering the seeds. You pat down the earth with care. Every day you water the spot; when it's needed, you add fertilizer. If you see a weed, you pull it out. You imagine what will one day grow there, and you send it your good intentions and pray for its survival. Eventually, with the help of the sun, all the nutrients in the earth, and your constant attention, a tree grows and, with its robust energy, bears fruit.

But when you see the tree has grown lemons, you're disappointed, maybe even annoyed.

"What's this? Lemons!" you complain. "I wanted cherries!"

Seems ridiculous, right? Well, oftentimes we focus our energy in a negative direction and then get disappointed when we don't like what grows out of it. Yet the rule is simple: What you plant in your life, you'll receive in return.

Job 14:1 (NIV) says,

Mortals, born of woman, are of few days and full of trouble.

If the Bible tells us that we all have trouble in our lives, it means sometimes bad things happen to good people. Why, then, would you add more heartache and more pain by planting things in your life that you don't want to see grow? Why do you plant a tree that will grow sour fruit?

I've learned whenever possible to plant good in my life so good will grow. I aim for sweetness, so sweetness will sprout.

I don't like to speak about my work with charitable causes because I don't do it for the publicity. But I'll make an exception, because this story clearly illustrates what I'm talking about.

A while back I was watching the news when I saw a story about an eighty-eight-year-old grandmother, Rosa Lee Ransby, raising seven grandkids in a small house in Newnan, Georgia. That kind of life is challenging enough, but, on top of the hardship and struggle, Rosa's house had burned to the ground.

Most people would have cursed their fate, railed against God, or just given up and let their life scatter like ashes. But Rosa Lee was too filled with love for her grandkids to think that way. Standing in front of the charred ruins of her home, she told the reporter in a surprisingly strong voice, "All I pray for is that my kids won't have to be separated from me."

I don't know where these kids' parents were, but it was clear as day—all they had in the entire world was the love and devotion of their remarkable grandma. Now they were facing homelessness. I felt the pain of this family's situation, so I got in touch with the television station and they gave me a way to contact Rosa Lee. It didn't take long to turn things around. First, I found her family a place to live, and then I built a house for them.

Since my mother had recently passed (this was 2009), I made the contribution in her memory. If Maxine had been alive, I know she would have been standing right beside me. It was her example of giving that first put me on this path.

I follow her steps. Maxine taught me that every good and perfect gift that you give finds its way back to you, not only in your life but also in your children's lives and for future generations. I believe this is a planet of harvest. The more positive and good you plant, the greater the harvest in your life, in your family's life, and in the lives of countless others.

Reaping what you sow is the simple law of nature.

When you express authentic kindness and compassion and bring people into the light, it will also be revealed in your own life and the lives of your children.

- What seeds are you planting and what fruits do you hope to harvest?

- Consider Galatians 6:7 (ESV): *For whatever one sows, that will he also reap.*

15

Separating Wheat from the Tares: The Parable of the Weeds

I T'S TRUE THAT we reap what we sow, but there are also times when negative stuff seems to sprout up randomly in our lives.

There's a reason for the turmoil, even though, at first glance, it may seem to have sprung from nowhere. One minute we're stepping deftly along the high ground, and the next minute we're thrown off-balance and tumbling down a steep hill. The questions to ask when this happens aren't "Why *me*?" or "Why now?" or even "Why do I deserve this?" but "What can I do about it?" and "What lesson can I learn?"

One of my favorite Bible stories illustrates this situation perfectly. The story told in Matthew 13:24–30 is about a farmer and his farmhands and the seeds that are planted in the field. In it, the kingdom of heaven may be compared to a man who sowed good seed in his field, but while his men were sleeping, his enemy came and sowed weeds among wheat. When the plants came up and bore grain, the weeds also appeared. Servants came to the house of the owner and said, "Master, did you not sow good seed in your field?"

"An enemy has done this," he answered.

The servants then asked, "Do you want us to go and gather them?"

"No, lest in gathering the weeds you root up the wheat along with them," the master responded. "Let both grow together until the harvest, and at harvest time I will tell the reapers, 'Gather the weed first and bind them in bundles to be burned, but gather the wheat into my barn.'"

In other words, once you learn to differentiate the good from the bad, the helpful from the useless, the supportive from the destructive, you can separate it, enjoy the fruits of your labor, and gain sustenance. You will be able to harvest your bounty in God's good time.

I've used this Bible story as guidance in my own life. For instance, I've been involved in relationships where I've acted honorably, cared about an individual, and treated the person with generosity and respect. Everything is moving along smoothly—and then there's some sort of betrayal. It can be devastating. I've found myself asking, *Where in the heck did this come from? It just makes no sense to me.* Tares are growing among the wheat.

My first inclination is just to pull up the whole mess and walk away from it. But as I've gained experience over the years and lived through this dynamic with different people,

I've learned to take certain steps before uprooting and discarding a friendship (or pulling the wheat from the tares). You don't just run away, give up on someone, and put that person out of your life. Sometimes you let them grow among the good, even though they may not get it. Keep them as part of your life and set a shining example.

But first, before making any decision whether to save or separate, I ask myself, *Did I do anything wrong?* If the answer is yes, I'm always ready to apologize; I never have a problem admitting when I've done something wrong. We're human; we're flawed. Mistakes are always possible. If it is my responsibility, without hesitation, I do whatever I can to right the problem.

If the answer is no, I first have to get over my disappointment. This is also a human reaction. Then, if there's really no excuse for this person's actions, no reason for him or her to have behaved in a destructive way, I accept the fact that our friendship has been violated. Finally, I make that decision about whether to keep this person in my life.

Some people come into our lives and we grow together forever in a healthy way. We're nourished by our companionship and mutual support. But other people come into our lives just for a season, a particular period, and then it's time to let go. In some ways, it's the law of human nature.

The signs are always there. If you see them, don't look away. Ask God if it's time to separate the wheat from the tares, and tune in to His answer.

• How did you react when you learned someone had betrayed you? How did you handle it?

• Can you apply the biblical parable about separating wheat from the tares to this situation and see what you might have done differently?

16

Clipping Wings

WHEN I WAS around thirteen I landed my first real job, at Ott's Pet Shop on Magazine Street in New Orleans. I walked into the store to buy food for Fifi and Pierre and thought, "Man, I'd love to work here." Without skipping a beat, I asked the owners, Miss Lynn and her brother Glenn, if they needed any part-time help. Lynn's "Yes!" rang in my ears like a beautiful bell.

I was one happy boy. I went straight home to tell my mother, and I can still remember her joining in my excitement. Big hugs. This was a real job, and she knew I was doing something that mattered to me.

What didn't matter to me was the fact that Ott's was twenty-five—literally *twenty-five*—blocks from my house! It's true I could have taken a streetcar, but I didn't want to waste the money. Instead, every day after school, I would trek down St. Charles Avenue, as happy as can be. Along the way, I'd pass huge, elegant Georgian homes, and I'd envision what my future would be like when I was older and living in a mansion.

Ott's wasn't grand like those mansions. The store was in an old building, but it had its own charm—mostly because of its animal inhabitants. The shop was remarkably narrow; a straight line from front to back like an arrow. On the right side were the cages and bags of food for dogs and cats, and on the left were all the fish, iguanas, reptiles, and assorted aquariums. My favorite place in Ott's was way in the back of the store, a little to the left. That's where the mice and birds lived.

I didn't like the mice much, but I loved, loved, loved those birds and spent as much time as I could with them. The really talkative parrot lived in the front of the shop and greeted customers when they walked in. I was mesmerized by that bird because I thought it had its freedom but stayed put.

"How do you keep her from flying away?" I asked Lynn.

She skillfully pulled the parrot's wings apart and pointed to where she had clipped off feathers. "Birds have thousands of feathers," she told me. "But if you clip these four right here, the bird can't fly."

Lynn wasn't the only one who wanted a bird grounded. Customers would bring their feathered pets into the shop and ask for the clipping. I would be the one to extend the bird's wings and hold them steady while Lynn calmly did the deed. Snip. Snip. Snip. Snip. It didn't hurt the bird at all. Best of all, I found out the feathers always grew back. Owners would have to do it from time to time, and not all of them came back. I like to think some of those birds got the chance to fly. Even if a bird is getting the best food in the world and lives in a beautiful home, if it can't fly it's missing out on a full life.

That's the way it is if our hearts are hurt and we get bitter; it's like our wings are clipped. You might look normal on the outside, lots of fancy feathers all over the place, and you might appear to be able to fly to the top of the earth, but if your feathers are damaged with the acid of bitterness, you'll be grounded.

How can you keep your flying feathers from being clipped? Be sure you release the bitterness in your heart. You'll know when you've done it because nothing will be holding you down.

- If I asked you if someone ever did something unforgivable to you, what would you say?

- One way to let go of bitterness is to stop dwelling and retelling. Let this be the last time you tell that story.

- Seek grace. Holding on to anything other than God's love and mercy makes it impossible to heal your wound.

- Consider Hebrews 12:15 (NIV): *See to it that no one falls short of the grace of God and that no bitter root grows up to cause trouble and defile many.*

17

Finding Faith
Without a Road Map

I LOVE MY LIFE now, but there were long years of financial struggle when, just to survive, I was forced to take
jobs that felt horrible to me. During this period I dreaded
waking up and going to work. I was sick of it: the commute, the people I worked with, what I had to do—
everything. But I had no choice. I was broke and living
paycheck to three-days-before-paycheck. I couldn't even
take a day off from the dreaded job for fear I would get
fired. I was terrified of ending up broke and homeless again.

On a typical day I would wake up at five in the morning
in order to make it to the office by nine. I walked three
miles just to get to the airport, where I would take a train to
downtown Atlanta. Next I would take a bus to Cobb County
and then walk about a half mile to my job at a collection
agency.

When I finally got to the office I dealt with eight hours

of nonstop negativity and heartache. My job was all about chasing down poor people and then tricking, lying, and manipulating them over the phone to get them to agree to be responsible for old collection accounts. Although some people were just trying to get away with not paying off their debts, I was aware that plenty of these folks had fallen on hard times, often through no fault of their own, and they simply couldn't afford to make payments. Still, I would have to go against my heart and try to talk them into paying. Every single time it made me feel sick inside. When someone agreed to the terms, I literally felt a bitterness rise in my throat.

I don't know whether my coworkers loved their jobs, but it seemed to me as if they didn't consider the people on the other end of the phone. I felt like they didn't think about them, and it seemed as if they only cared about one thing: "winning" and getting their commissions. If someone said yes to a debt payment, they would slam their palms down on a round bell—*Ding! Ding! Ding!*—smile widely, and give a series of high-five slaps. My coworkers appeared to thrive on other people's misery. For me, it was a very, very sad situation.

I couldn't help but feel disheartened. God had placed all these dreams and hopes within me. I wanted to help people, bring joy into their lives, guide them to dream higher, and yet I was stuck here. Instead of going higher, I was making lives even more miserable. I had no idea how I was ever going to realize my dreams to better others as well as myself. To have a dream of something bigger and not see a way of getting there felt like death to me. I pleaded, "Dear God, why would you give me so much hope and not make a way?"

Psalms 119:105 (KJV) says,

Thy word is a lamp unto my feet,
and a light unto my path.

This particular verse inspired me to ask God to be the lamp unto my feet and show me the path out of darkness, to show me the way to get to where I knew I was supposed to be.

"Please," I prayed, "make the path plain so I can see where to go. Show me my next steps."

Once I became quiet and tuned in, God's answer came through. But as is so often the case, it wasn't what I had asked for. The message said, "True faith begins when there's no path in front of you and no road map."

Wow. I got it. It clicked.

Now I understood. I had been asking God why he gave me dreams but kept me stuck in a job that felt so wrong for me. I wanted Him to make my path plain and put me on a direct route to the light. But I had it wrong. Everything you do, moment to moment, *is* the path. It's about how you handle the obstacles put in your path. How you live your life no matter what you're doing. When you have faith, you don't need a road map; faith lights the way.

I was going to get there.

• Consider a frustrating situation in your life and describe what makes you feel so frustrated.

• Next, ask yourself: "Where am I in this?" Then ask, "God, where are YOU in this?" The answers might surprise you.

18

———

Tuning In

WHEN I DON'T hear God's voice it means something is wrong; life is amiss. It's like looking at a picture that's slightly out of focus, watching events that don't quite add up, or walking a few steps behind the beat. Intuition shuts down, and I feel as if I'm moving through my day without a compass.

It happened to me pretty recently. For six or eight months, I was waking up in the morning, watching the news first thing, and being fully captivated by our country's drama and polarization. Political theater can be addictive. Admittedly, there was pretty electrifying news out there, and I allowed myself to become absorbed in it. Around the same time, I was also dealing with my everyday business and allowing myself to react to events rather than sorting through the issues and responding to what really mattered. In other words, I got completely caught up in the material world. I put my soul on the back burner. I didn't make time for prayer.

I was adrift because I had stopped checking in to my

heart and soul for answers. I wasn't tuned in. During this time, I found myself experiencing high levels of frustration, aggravation, nitpicking, and disappointment. From the outside, it would have seemed that things were going pretty well, but inwardly I felt something was wrong. I certainly wasn't feeling happy or in balance.

What did I do?

The first step was simply realizing I was out of whack. Some people have to hit rock bottom before they can see where they're standing. They have to be lost before they are found. I'm grateful that for me, over the years, I've become more attuned. I pick up on internal signals when they alert me that it's time to reset. In this particular instance, I knew where to go; I needed to reconnect with my spiritual longing.

There is no secret formula for getting back there since it really is our natural state. It's simple. For starters, I stopped turning on the television first thing in the morning. Instead, I made the time to sit quietly and speak to God. I opened to sharing our moments together in prayer. I checked in to hear from myself, to ask questions or request guidance, to listen to my thoughts and to hear what God may be saying to me.

In this way I'm able to begin each day with a reverence for God and His blessings. It sets the tone and puts my step in sync. I begin from a place of perspective. With my practice of prayer and meditation in the mornings, I'm more likely to stay tuned to a higher frequency and keep my priorities in place for the rest of the day. It's my ticket to ride life with presence and awareness.

I may not be on track every single day, but I'm not likely to miss the station altogether.

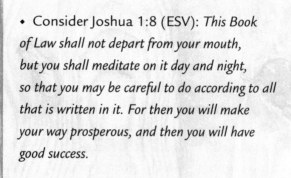

 • Consider Joshua 1:8 (ESV): *This Book of Law shall not depart from your mouth, but you shall meditate on it day and night, so that you may be careful to do according to all that is written in it. For then you will make your way prosperous, and then you will have good success.*

19

Unlocking the Secret of
a Closed Door

WHEN I WAS in my thirties I had the chance to create a television show based on my characters and experiences for one of the big three networks. A high-powered producer wanted to work with me. It promised to rocket me to the constellations, fueled by star power. It seemed as if the sky was the limit. But intuitively, I knew something odd was going on. The project felt empty, dark, and, in some ways, hopeless. One thing was clear: I would have to give up creative control. That's a big deal for me, and I knew in my heart it was the wrong way to go.

Still, my agents—well, *everybody*—was telling me this was the giant twenty-four-karat-gold, diamond-studded door. I should grab the handle, turn it, and barge through without hesitation. Huge success awaited me on the other side.

But then . . . the door *shut*.

The whole deal fell apart.

People around me were all doom and gloom.

"Too bad, Tyler."

"What a loss."

"This could have been your big break, TP."

"So sorry for the letdown."

Honestly? I was happy. All along I knew the deal had a time limit on it, and I was hoping the time would run out. And then it did. I was glad God had closed that door. Before long, I ended up taking a different route, staying in control by writing and producing my own shows, and along the way my life opened to higher.

If you're in a similar situation and you feel like doors are closing to you, it's human to feel frustrated, maybe even hopeless. Let me offer what I call the Maze Message. It might help inspire you to move toward your dream.

Think about it this way: In a maze you enter at one end with the objective to exit somewhere else. As you move along, you might hit a dead end and be forced to reconsider your route. You'll be made to choose a different way to go.

Taking another path doesn't mean you won't reach your goal. It just means you need to find another way. Be patient. If you keep moving, and stay open to other turns, alternate routes, and expanded possibilities, you'll eventually get to where you want to go.

It's important when you're in a maze, as in life, to remember and keep in mind where you've been, and to learn from your past. You can't expect to make your dream a reality by going in the same wrong direction, hitting the same dead ends, again and again. I'm not saying to give up on your dream. I'm saying try getting there a different way. Same maze, same dream, different route.

Sure, it can be frustrating. But so what? Vow to persevere. Don't stop just because one door is closed. You have to know that if God wanted you to go through a particular door, the handle would have turned and the door would have opened.

Have faith that there is another door awaiting you somewhere else.

When the right door opens, don't hesitate.

Walk through it.

- Have you ever tried to beat down a closed door?

- Consider Revelation 3:8 (NLT*): *I know all the things you do, and I have opened a door for you that no one can close.*

---

* New Living Translation

PART THREE

Branching Out

WITHOUT STURDY ROOTS A TREE can't survive; it won't have the energy to grow tall, spread its branches, and bear fruit. I thank God my soul's roots are deep and strong, and have given me the chance to branch out and inspire others to climb. That's always been my dream: to empower people to live a better life, find happiness, heal from hurts, open to higher, and, along the way, know they can trust God to hold them.

The branches of faith gave me support so I could stretch higher. They led me to the light. The only way I could have healed was to trust fully in God's messages, grab hold, and keep climbing. As you find God by ascending limb by limb, you may have to face your old patterns.

Before you can climb higher, anger, disappointment, resentment, hurt, and fear may rise up and ask to be heard. Some branches may be too damaged to support you. You will have to let go of those. Other branches may have the potential to lift you higher. Have faith that those branches will be strengthened by your growth. Know there are plenty more available for the climb.

20

Looking in the Right Place

ON ONE PARTICULARLY sticky summer's day I was trying to stay cool while one of my closest friends was describing the many times people had disappointed or betrayed her. "They've done awful things to me." She sighed and then went on to explain how several family members and friends had let her down and broken her heart. "I just wish they would be better people," she said.

In the midst of her story, I suggested we take a walk in my backyard and breathe some fresh air. Now, you have to know this particular friend of mine, whom I love, *hates* the heat—and it was a *very* hot day—but I was insistent.

"Come on," I said. "Let's go outdoors."

"Really? You trying to torture me?" was her response. But I coaxed her good-naturedly, and she reluctantly agreed.

Once we were outside, we were immediately hit with a blast of stifling air, the kind that offers a fiery wallop to the skin. I could tell she was super uncomfortable, dabbing her forehead and upper lip, but still, we continued to stroll around the yard. With each slow and sweaty step she continued complaining about "those awful people."

When we were standing right under the sun's blazing rays, in a spot where the grass looked especially vibrant, I interrupted her midsentence.

"What do you think of my lawn?" I asked, spreading my palms out in front of me, panning the property like a camera.

She took in the yard. "Wow, I love it!" she said. "It's gorgeous . . . just like lush velvet!"

Then she looked up and squinted at the sun's rays beating directly down on us. "But it's so unbelievably hot right here. Let's cool off under the tree." She pointed to a sturdy oak with its leafy promise of shade and started walking toward the bench directly under it.

"Oh, no, no," I said. "Let's stay here and cool off."

"Cool off? We can't cool off here!" she said, her voice getting testy.

"Right," I agreed. "But didn't you just say you loved the grass?"

"I did," she replied.

"Then why don't we stay here and enjoy it?"

"Because it's hot, and grass can't cool us off!"

Who could argue with her reasoning? Not me. So we walked over to the oak tree, sat on the shaded bench, and breathed in the relief.

"Now, you see, *this* is what I need," she said with a sigh.

I paused for a moment, allowing my heart to open wider—and continued our conversation.

"You say you love the grass. So why do you get mad at it

when it can't give you the shade you want and need?" I asked.

Her forehead creased with confusion so I went on. "Whether people are born one way and it's their nature, or they grow into a particular way because of their life's circumstances, they are exactly who they are. Stop wishing they could be someone else."

I carried on with this train of thought, picking up steam along the way. "The next time you get upset with someone because he can't be who you want him to be, remind yourself of the grass," I suggested. "Don't bother getting mad at a blade of grass because it's not a tree. Appreciate the grass for what it is. Let it provide for you what it can, but don't expect more than it can give."

My friend finally understood the point I was making. She looked me in the eyes and shot a wide smile my way. "True!"

It's an important lesson for all of us. Life gets easier and happier when we let people be whoever they truly are. Stop expecting them to give you what they don't have or don't know how to give. In the same way grass can't give shade because that's not its purpose, some people are not made to be generous or kind.

Don't waste your energy being frustrated with folks who are like the grass. Spend more time with people who are like trees. You'll be surprised to discover how much more comfort you'll find.

• Consider Psalms 37:1–4 (ESV): *Fret not yourself because of evildoers; be not envious of wrongdoers! For they will soon fade like the grass and wither like the green herb. Trust in the Lord, and do good; dwell in the land and befriend faithfulness. Delight yourself in the Lord and he will give you the desires of your heart.*

• Do you have a friend who is always letting you down? Why are you still friends? Do you think it's their problem or yours? Why?

21

Seeing Through Time

I'M WAITING UNTIL *the time is right.*

You've heard people say those words and you've probably said them yourself. Honestly? I've said them, too. I always want to reach the next level, but I can find a million reasons why I'm not ready to make the push to get there.

Staying put was exactly what I had in mind in 2001 when I bought a building for my business. It was a historic turn-of-the-century brick warehouse in downtown Atlanta. I loved the character of the old property and its central location. But I knew it had some major shortcomings. It didn't have enough storage space, parking, or room to create all my projects. Neighbors complained about the lights, noise, and traffic. They were annoyed that my employees were taking up precious parking spaces on the street. Plus, the neighborhood was a little rough, and almost every morning I would drive up to find new gang graffiti scrawled across the building. I owned the property outright, but soon I knew my business was outgrowing the building. It was bursting at the seams! There was more going on than the walls could handle. Still, even with all these issues, I wanted to hang on.

The problems kept intensifying, and one day my lawyer called and strongly suggested that I take a look at Greenbriar Campus. The property consisted of several buildings on a sixty-acre lot that was only around twenty minutes from Atlanta's downtown.

When I first drove up to Greenbriar Campus, I didn't even get out of my truck. "No way!" I said to myself. "Who needs *all* this?" In that moment, I couldn't fathom what I would do with all that property. I didn't want to make the push.

I turned the key and drove off, not even taking a second glance in my rearview mirror.

But that night I couldn't sleep. Suddenly my mind was ready to wrestle with the potential, and my soul, sparked by my imagination, started praying about the possibilities. Unable to sleep because my mind was racing a mile a minute, I got in my truck and drove through the pitch dark back to Greenbriar Campus.

I pulled up to the property and just sat there with the headlights on for a few minutes, stunned that I'd found myself back here. Then I got out, walked up to the wrought iron gate, saw it was padlocked with a thick chain, tried it with no luck, and stood still, quietly peering through the gate.

It was a scene out of an apocalyptic movie. Silver paint peeled and unfurled like tape off the main building. Weeds grew with such maniacal tenacity, they wound and weaved and reached the tops of the windows and doors. Old newspapers, bottles, plastic bags, and Styrofoam cups were scattered everywhere.

In the dead of night, with a cacophony of crickets chirping, my mind continued to race with possibilities. All my convenient excuses were telling me to just stay put in my lovely brick building, but . . .

I took a big breath and then slowly and steadily exhaled, and asked God, "Well, what am I supposed to do?"

I stayed open.

"God, if this is your will, I need you to make it clear to me."

No sooner had I asked than my gaze settled once again on the wrought iron gate: "What's this?" It looked like scripture had been cut from a Bible and taped to a space between the bars. The papers were discolored and fragile, but in the glow of the truck's headlights I managed to read some of the verses.

And there, right in front of me, was one of my all-time favorite verses, Psalms 91:1 (ESV):

He who dwells in the shelter of the Most High will abide in the shadow of the Almighty.

Tears rolled down my cheeks. In that instant, any doubt, any hesitation, was instantly washed away. I told myself, "I must to do this."

The timing still felt wrong, but the voice of God within me said, "Move now. Do it now. Don't wait. Push." And so, in my head and heart, it was already a done deal.

First thing the next morning I called the owner.

"I'm interested in Greenbriar Campus," I told him in a steady voice.

"Too late," he told me. "A pastor from New Orleans is buying the property and turning it into his church. It's no longer for sale."

My heart sank, but I didn't hesitate. The next call I made was to the only New Orleans pastor I thought would be in a position to buy the place, Bishop Paul Morton. He also happened to be the pastor of the church where I saw that gold-leafed tree as a boy.

"Are you interested in Greenbriar Campus?" I asked the bishop.

"Yes, how did you know?" He sounded surprised. "I was just there a day ago."

I told Bishop Morton what had happened, how I had returned to the campus late at night, asked God for a sign, and then found the scripture.

"This has got to be the Lord speaking to us," he said. He paused for a long moment and then asked, "Would you consider buying thirty acres and the buildings? I don't want the whole sixty-something acres."

"Sure," I said without taking a breath. "That's *exactly* what I want!" With all the pieces coming together—Bishop Morton and his church, my business and me—we were a match, you might say, "made in heaven."

What's more, during this process I learned a lesson about timing and faith that I will never forget. If you're living by faith, you never have to wait for the timing to be right. In fact, the two don't go together. They're not the same thing.

Waiting for the so-called right time is waiting for an illusion to become real. There's just no such thing. The right time can't be found on a calendar or a clock.

Living by faith means stepping away from any fear and discomfort holding us back.

It's about tuning in to your soul.

It's about trusting the message.

When you hear God give you the go-ahead, don't let your mind make up excuses by saying it's not the right time. Know that the time is right now.

Surprisingly, it wasn't too long before I had to rely on this message again. God offered yet another opportunity to push and grow.

When we took over Greenbriar Campus, I thought, "This is *it;* we're in our forever home." I remember telling one of our producers, "We'll never outgrow this space." But guess what? Not two years into it, the staff was falling all over one another again. There wasn't enough room! Once again, my first reaction (as in "reactive") was to stay put. I listed the excuses for staying: It's convenient, right on the bus line. Everybody is familiar and comfortable in the space. I definitely don't want the hassle of moving, and so forth. But once again, all kinds of trouble started to come my way—missteps, miscommunications, and mis-understandings. God was prodding me to push to the next level.

Once I raised my heart to the light, I knew it was time to leave Greenbriar Campus; I was even ready to move to a site outside the city. I phoned the mayor of Atlanta to let him know my decision.

"Don't make your final decision yet," he pleaded. "First you have to see something. Please meet me at Fort McPherson Army Base."

The only thing I knew about the army base was that it was a stop on the MARTA (Metropolitan Atlanta Rapid Transit Authority). Years ago, when I worked at the collection agency, I used to pass the MARTA station on my long commute. Now here I was, decades later, meeting Atlanta's mayor at the historic military base. When I got there, I climbed into his car. He informed me that the base was for sale and then said, "I'm not going to utter a word. Let's just go for a ride."

And, boy, did we ride—on and on and on . . . and on. The car passed building after building, along miles of land. I was impressed, but I sat back in my seat and listened for God's directive. Surprisingly, I didn't have to wait long. There was the familiar voice. It was saying, "This is *it!*"

Time to move again.

It was the right move to make. Business is booming. Right now we're putting the finishing touches on our twelfth soundstage.

* Do you remember an instance when you waited for the "right time" and the opportunity passed you by?

22

———

Releasing Filters

I'VE NEVER LIKED coffee, but Aunt Mae loved the stuff. She prepared her coffee by grinding dark beans in a hand-turned mill until they were just the right consistency, then she brewed it without a filter. Let me tell you, it was strong—*very* strong—coffee. It had bite, but it was also sweet. Mae's coffee lingered in the air and on your taste buds long after the cup was emptied.

As an adult, I've seen coffee made in conventional ways and know that in most cases filters are used in the process. Filtered coffee, as it turns out, is weaker and often has a bitter and forgettable taste. It's not at all like Aunt Mae's hearty, bold cup of java.

The same is true in life. The more filters we put on our lives, the less likely we're our boldest, fullest, strongest, and most memorable selves.

I can't help but think about my son, Aman, when it comes to unfiltered living. My little boy is only a toddler, and so he exists in our world with a kind of holiness. No filters. No shame. No self-consciousness, just pure presence, pleasure, and innocence. On a recent vacation, I watched him taking in the beach for the first time. He was totally absorbed in the experience. He put his feet in the sand and wiggled his toes. He bent down, picked up a clump of sand in his hands, and examined the grains with his full-on attention. He rubbed his fingers together, studying the texture with concentration. This simple beach, an experience in totally unfiltered joy for my little boy.

Like Aman, we're all born with the ability to experience life full-on. We come into this world with purity, innocence, and holiness. I believe that's why Jesus said,

> *Truly, I say to you, unless you turn and become like children, you will never enter the kingdom of heaven.*

But as we grow older, that age of innocence departs. We dim our experience to the natural world around us, get hardened, distracted, numbed, judgmental—and reactive—often in a negative or fearful way.

Rather than approaching new experiences with bright-eyed wonder, we look at them through the gauze of our accumulated personal history. We've experienced relationships with our family, lovers, friends, neighbors, and colleagues. We've found love. We've experienced betrayal. We've felt sadness. We've found pain. And all these various experiences and emotional reactions to them create filters over our lives. Each and every filter numbs us to living a juicy, full-throttled life in the present—in the here and now.

So are you going to choose filtered, watered-down, bitter coffee while you hold on to your past? Or are you willing to brew your mind and heart without filters and take fresh sips of life at full strength, so your whole soul can savor its robust nectar? Can you drink in your days, paying attention to what you experience, and release the reactive filters that keep you from living with presence and loving awareness?

I say, if you want to experience life with an open and alive heart, wake up and smell the coffee!

Make mine unfiltered.

• Think about an event in your life that wounded you so deeply that you created a filter to protect yourself. What's keeping you from releasing that filter?

• Affirmation: "The past is gone, the future uncertain. Today is now and I face it head-on." Even better, write your own affirmation that will help you to let go of a filter.

• Consider Philippians 3:13 (NASB*):
Brethren, I do not regard myself as having laid hold of it yet; but one thing I do: forgetting what lies behind and reaching forward to what lies ahead.

---

* New American Standard Bible

23

Guarding Your Heart

YES, WE ENTER this world with a pure heart that holds no judgment, but keeping that childlike innocence and trust isn't easy. Unless you work at it with conscious awareness, it's more likely to be impossible. As I said before, filters prevent it. Another obstacle? Well, life happens, and we're not always sailing a calm sea. Trust me when I tell you, I've had to ride out raging storms that have wreaked havoc in my personal and professional life. I've been there big-time. You've probably been there, too.

I want to tell you something about these moments when your heart is breaking. First, learn the lesson in it. Understand there's power in the feeling. There's a well-known quotation: "They may forget what you said, but they will never forget how you made them feel." I put it slightly differently: I don't remember every moment in my life, but I do remember every moment that changed my life.

Acknowledge the pain, but then try to take a few steps away so you can get some distance. Once you have space, try to look at your situation more clearly, without your reactive mind. Try to change your perspective. See how your present circumstance can work for your own good. *It will.*

Once you do this, see how your predicament can be used as nourishment for your growth. Ask yourself, "Why did this happen? What's my part in the chain of events? How would I do it differently next time?" When you arrive at the answers to the questions, it will be easier for you to accept what happened, forgive, recover, and move on.

Secondly, and this is just as important as the first step, you must not let that person or event harden your heart. What do I mean by that? Well, if you are a giver and someone misuses your gift, don't stop giving. Give to someone else. If you are a person who loves people and someone you love hurts you, don't stop loving. Love someone else. Eventually you will find people who appreciate your kindness and love.

Many people are unable to accept a kind heart. They don't trust it. They can't take it in. Most of the time, it's not their fault. It's probably the result of their experiences on their life's journey. Some people have their hearts hardened in childhood; some have shut down because their hearts were broken later in life, and they never worked to heal themselves. In both instances, they've been conditioned to shut down. But don't let their reaction shut *you* down. Don't let it damage your heart. Don't walk away from your willingness to be vulnerable and loving.

Why is this so important?

The Bible answers this question in Proverbs 4:23 (NIV):

*Above all else, guard your heart, for
everything you do flows from it.*

You can lose every material thing in this world that you
own, but don't let anybody change your naturally sweet
heart.

Guard it with your life.

• Speaking from your own experience,
why do you think God wants you to
guard your heart?

• Consider 2 Timothy 1:6 (ESV): *For this
reason I remind you to fan into flame the gift of
God, which is in you through the laying on
of my hands.*

24

Trusting Your Soul GPS

THESE DAYS, WHEN we're driving somewhere and we don't know the way, we program our car's GPS and trust it's going to lead us to our destination. All we have to do is say something like, "This is where I want to go," and the GPS replies, "Okay, start here . . . turn right here . . . turn left here."

I did this not too long ago because I was invited to a church in Gardena, California, and all I knew about the area was that it was somewhere in the South Bay part of Los Angeles. Since I didn't know how to get there, I had to trust every direction my GPS gave—the right turns, the left turns, the roads to get on and off. I knew if I didn't pay strict attention, if I got distracted or was tempted to ignore the GPS, I would probably get lost.

I wasn't driving too long before the navigator's voice led me off the freeway and into a pretty sketchy part of town. I was riding along gripping the wheel. It was getting pretty dark and I was passing gang signs along the way. Unnerved,

I began speeding up to make all the lights. As soon as the light changed, I was on it.

Suddenly I see flashing lights in my rearview mirror. I pull over, and a police officer comes up to the door and gives my car the once-over. I can read his expression. I know what he's thinking: "What's *this* car doing in this neighborhood?" I lower the window, and I'm happy to see that he recognizes me pretty quickly.

"What are *you* doing around here?" he asks.

So I explain where I want to go and end by saying, "My navigation system took me this way."

"Oh, yeah." He rolls his eyes. "Your navigation will definitely take you this way, but this a rougher route. Just make a left, get back on the thruway, and follow your GPS from there."

Well, I did just that, but as is often the case in my life, I learned a lesson and I'm grateful for it. The first lesson was this: Once you tune back in to the navigational device, you'll get directions on how to correct your route.

That got me to thinking about our life's journey, and then I had another realization: We all come equipped with our personal Soul GPS. We may not know exactly where we are going, how to get there, or the roads to take. That's why we have to trust our Soul GPS to help us reach our destination: our destiny. All we can do is put in the address of where we want to go (our dream) and then pay attention to our inner ride. We have to follow with full trust what our Soul GPS is telling us to do. Of course, it's not always an easy ride or a simple route.

The GPS won't tell you if you're going to come upon a roadblock, construction, or a sketchy neighborhood. It won't tell you if a pedestrian is going to dart out into the street and you'll have to slam on the brakes. It can't tell you if you're going to be stuck behind a garbage truck. It won't let you know if the car right in front of you is going to break down, have a fender bender, or just travel at a snail's pace. And it won't tell you if a road worker is about to put up a sign that says DETOUR AHEAD.

It's the same with your Soul GPS. Your job is to be clear and set your goal—your destination—in your heart. Be direct about what you want to do and where you want to go—and then drive on. No matter what route you end up taking, God will get you there. He sees what's ahead.

God is like a satellite that navigates us around our lives. He's telling us which direction to take and what turns to make. But God's directions are like the GPS in your car: You have to pay attention to them or you're going to get lost. You may have to backtrack. You may have to take a different route, one you hadn't planned on taking. You may not make it exactly at the time you thought you would reach your destination because of unforeseen variables.

But stick to your Soul GPS.

Envision your destination. Drive toward your dream.

Trust God's navigation.

You'll get to where He wants you to be.

It's *your* fate.

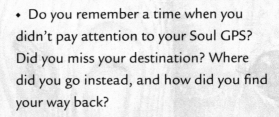

• Do you remember a time when you didn't pay attention to your Soul GPS? Did you miss your destination? Where did you go instead, and how did you find your way back?

• If you find that you're "stuck" on your life's journey, accept that there's more than one way to reach your destination. Tune in to your Soul GPS to find another route.

• Try this affirmation: "I'm on the road to meet my dream."

25

———

Answering God's Questions

I LOVE IT WHEN God asks questions in the Bible. Of course, he doesn't ask for Himself. He already knows everything. He asks us because He wants us to dig deeper, unearth the truth, and discover the answer for ourselves. Only when we make an unconditional effort to search within ourselves will our discovery be revealed as a true and lasting treasure.

In Exodus 4:2 God asks Moses: "What is it that you have in your hand?"

Even though Moses knows he's holding a staff, he's not aware of the staff's potential and power. God's question encourages him to discover its hidden abilities.

Like the staff in Moses's hand, the very skill with which we need to climb higher is already in our grasp. The sturdy and supportive branch is right there.

When I was growing up I knew great things were going to unfold in my life, but I didn't have a clue as to how I was going to get there. I didn't realize at the time that the staff in my hand was the gift of storytelling and writing.

I started writing to deal with my childhood abuse and to help me get over it. I began putting my thoughts on paper because I saw a show on Oprah where she said it was "cathartic" to write things down. Being from a substandard public school system, I didn't even know what "cathartic" meant. I had to look it up. So I started writing, but I didn't even realize I was writing a play. I just used different characters' names so that if someone found my pages, they wouldn't know I was writing about myself. But eventually I let a close and trusted friend read what I'd written, and he said, "Man, this is a really good play."

I thought, "Wow, maybe this *is* a play." That's how it started for me. At first I didn't know I had the gift to tell stories, I just knew it felt right. But once I discovered this power, I nourished and cultivated it. With practice, writing grew to be a stronger and important part of me. To this day it sustains my business and supports my way of life. It is who I am.

When God asks, "What is that you have in your hand?" it's up to us to find the answer. Everyone's answer is different. But there is something we all share.

Everything is already inside you.

All you have to do is mine it.

Dig down deep and discover your thing.

♦ What is the staff in your hand? What is inside you that you've yet to tap?

• How will you use your special power to make your life and the lives of others better?

26

Showing Love

I'VE ALWAYS DISLIKED it when someone says to me, "You have no idea how much I love you." It doesn't matter if it's said within a romantic relationship or by friends or family members. What I hear instead is, "I have an excuse for not showing you my full heart."

Every soul needs to experience authentic, no-holds-barred love. That's why it's important to be vulnerable, to be exposed, to be out there leading with your open heart. No excuses. Too many of us worry about getting hurt, so we block our true feelings, protect our hearts, and hide behind "You have no idea how much I love you."

I understand how tough it is to let yourself be vulnerable. If you're holding back, you might have been hurt in the past and are defending against it happening again.

Or maybe you feel overwhelmed. Maybe you're very busy; with so much going on, you can't make room to be fully present—to show love and appreciation—or so you think. In that case, maybe you're not willing to make love a priority. Maybe you fear that love won't be enough.

Am I disappointed when I hear those words from somebody?

Honestly, yes. When I love, I try to love and give fully, and I hope that anybody who loves me will open their heart and do the same. That's why if you say, "You have no idea how much I love you," I'll say, *"Show* me."

• There's more to love than just saying it. What are five ways you show love in your relationships?

27

Lighting the Way

BEFORE FLASHLIGHTS WERE standard features on mobile phones, I used my cellphone's regular light. If I had to get up and walk somewhere in the middle of the night and folks were sleeping nearby, I would turn on my phone and be careful to keep the light directed toward my feet because I didn't want to wake anyone.

One night when I was on one of my cellphone-lit walks, I suddenly thought, "Wow, this is the lamp unto my feet." I had only enough light to see one or two steps in front of me. I couldn't see all the way to my destination. But as long as I kept the light on my feet, I was able to move forward and navigate safely around the house and get to where I needed to be.

Sometimes faith is like that. You can't really see the whole picture. You don't know how your life is going to end up or even the way it will unfold. All you have is the light right at your feet, taking you step by step, moment by moment.

When you live with faith, His grace shines upon your

pathway and guides you. You can travel through your life's journey with sure-footed confidence. Jesus is our true light, and he came to bring us out of darkness. Without Christ, we would be left wandering aimlessly in the dark.

• Where do you find the light to lead you out of darkness?

• Did you ever learn a lesson you've never forgotten when you were stumbling around without hope or direction?

28

Flying Through Rough Air

THERE WAS A time in my life, years before I learned how to fly a plane, when the last thing I wanted to do was sit inside one. Being six foot six and gliding through the air stuffed inside a metal tube and squeezed into a cramped seat was unappealing enough on the physical level. But intellectually, too, I didn't understand how all that weight could stay aloft. When I don't have knowledge, when I can't understand something, I don't feel safe.

On top of that, I had a fear of turbulence; any kind of shaking or rough air would set my nerves on edge. My imagination would leap to the absolute worst outcome. I didn't know the pilots personally—what had they been doing before they took their seats in the cockpit? What if they were having a bad day? What if they'd been drinking or doing drugs? My panicky thoughts took on a life of their own. I felt out of control, something I hate.

All this was on my mind during a rainy and foggy drive years ago from my home to the airport in Atlanta. I needed to be in New Jersey for the opening of a new play and, despite my reluctance, flying in a small private jet was the only way I could get there on time.

When I arrived at the airport, I was a shaky mess. I warned the pilot about my condition before we took off.

"You've got a nervous flier on board," I said. "What's the weather like up there?"

"It's rough down low," the pilot said. "But great up high."

I tilted my head skyward and, frankly, it didn't look so great up high. Storm clouds were swirling and the rain was relentless, but I bit the bullet and got on the plane.

I buckled in tightly. After we took off, a mighty turbulence tossed the plane around almost immediately. It was as if we were sitting on individual trampolines. I was completely terrified. When I looked out the window all I could see was a thick wall of charcoal gray—zero visibility. I was white-knuckling it, grabbing hold of the seat's armrest. "Jesus, Jesus, Jesus," I prayed.

Fearing for my life and hoping we weren't going to crash, I was just about to ask the pilot to land and let me off the plane when, suddenly, we broke through the clouds. We were climbing. Blinding sunlight pierced my eyes like a luminous blade. From that moment on, the flight was easy; I couldn't even feel the plane moving. We landed in New Jersey as smooth as butter under bright blue skies.

Days later, when I thought about my harrowing trip, I realized that flying through rough weather is a lot like making it through life. Sometimes there are lots of gray clouds, unsettling vibrations, turbulence, and plenty of nail-biting moments. Sometimes it can be so frightening, you may want to turn around and go back. Sometimes you have to climb through the clouds to reach a higher altitude for your own safety.

You may not be ready to go higher, but just as air traffic control had to give us permission before the pilot could climb above the turbulence, I'm giving you permission to climb.

Stop living your life so low.

You may not be able to see it yet, but the sun is shining brightly up there.

It may not be so easy to cut through the clouds.

You'll need to navigate carefully to ascend.

But you will.

Use prayer as your fuel.

You have just been given permission to climb higher.

◆ Consider a fear you have. It could be flying, heights, being alone, speaking in public—whatever frightens you. What's keeping you from climbing higher? What are you willing to do to overcome it?

29

Leaving the Nest

WHILE ON A visit to Wyoming, I was taking in the magnificent view of the Grand Tetons off in the distance when my gaze was suddenly drawn to an eagle soaring high in the sky. Its massive wingspan and elegant silent flight took my breath away and filled my soul with a feeling of grace. It was the first time in my life I'd ever seen an eagle, and the sight of it evoked the memory of a pastor's sermon I had heard years before.

"Mamma eagles are fierce," the pastor had said. "They're so fierce that—ready or not—they'll push their babies from the nest to force them to fly."

"This eagle had to go through all that in order to soar," I said to myself. Throughout the day I thought about what the eagle had endured.

In the evening when I returned to my cabin, I was still feeling the soul-opening experience of seeing that bird in flight. I took out my laptop and did some research about eagles. And this is what I learned: Mamma eagles do *not* push their young ones from the nest!

I'm not going to say the pastor lied, but I will say he didn't do his research thoroughly. As I read on, I learned several more fascinating facts about eagles that got me to thinking about life—yours and mine.

Eagles build the biggest nests of any bird: deep, comfy, and roomy. For weeks, the adult eagle brings food to the nest, and the little chicks have no worries at all. They have everything they need to survive and thrive. No wonder they don't want to leave.

But the mamma eagle knows best. When she deems it's time for her little ones to take flight, she no longer puts food into their open mouths. Instead, she'll fly above and around the nest with the food in her own beak. Her babies will have to leave their cushy nest and fly in order to grab the food and get the nourishment they crave.

As I contemplated nature's aerial choreography, I reflected on my own life, the times I was in a comfortable place where all my needs were being met. During these cushy periods, there was no reason for me to go any further, no push to reach higher.

But inevitably, just as I was getting a little lazy and relaxing into a cozy place, my world would get turned around. A business would change. A job would go awry. A relationship would turn rocky.

I'm of the opinion that during these difficult times God knows it's time for us to leave the nest. He's allowing discomfort, so that we can move on to our next mission in life, our next hope—our next level—our next dream.

For years, I didn't understand this rule of life. I was always resisting change. I used to be so stubborn that a house would have to burn down to get me out of it. Now I know better. I'm glad to say that I have become sensitive to when it's time to move on. I can read the signs, whether they're obvious or subtle, and usually get going without needing to experience heaviness or turmoil.

Of course, nobody likes change. But if it happens to you, try not to be angered, afraid, or bitter. If God has allowed you to become uncomfortable in your situation, know that it's probably time for you to move on.

But that's not the end of the story—for the baby eagle or for us. If the young chick's attempt at flying isn't going well, his mamma is right below him to offer him a sense of security and to prevent him from tumbling to the ground.

Think about yourself as a baby eagle leaving a comfortable nest. If things start becoming difficult while you're taking flight, don't be afraid.

Spread your wings and fly.

God's got you.

He won't let you fall.

+ Describe a situation in your life that became so uncomfortable, you had to change course. What did you learn from it?

+ Consider Isaiah 40:31 (ESV): *But they who wait for the Lord shall renew their*

strength; they shall mount up with wings
like eagles; they shall run and not be weary;
they shall walk and not faint.

30

Breaking Patterns

IT'S NOT UNUSUAL for me to take on the role of counselor with my close friends. I've certainly had my share of ups and downs, so I feel like I've gained a pretty clear and wide perspective. On one such evening of camaraderie I was speaking with a good buddy who was feeling lower than a blade of grass. His damaged self-esteem and internal darkness had been following him like a shadow for much of his life.

To help him figure out why he was so melancholy, I asked him to try to focus on those times when he felt especially bleak and hopeless.

He didn't have to search long before he found his answer. "This may sound strange, but some of my worst times are when I'm with my girlfriend," he admitted. "She's mean and disrespectful to me, and whenever I'm around her I feel humiliated, weak, and worthless."

Then he went on to describe the numerous times he felt her contempt. The words she used and her belittling tone, as he described it, made him feel as if he were getting slapped in the face.

After some long and deep conversations, my friend was finally able to understand that he was in a toxic relationship. To those who knew him, it may have seemed as obvious as seeing your own reflection in a mirror, but sometimes when you're burning in the intense fire of a situation, it's tough to see what's feeding the flames of destruction. You need to be able to take a step back and take a good look at the entire scene for yourself.

My friend went on to make a discovery that changed his life forever. He understood that the relationship he had with this woman was exactly the kind of relationship he'd had with his family during his childhood.

"When I was growing up, there were a lot of people in my life who told me that I was nothing. I was never going to be anything. I was a completely hopeless human being with no potential to accomplish anything," he recalled. "Anytime I reached for something, my aspiration was ridiculed.

"Those same childhood feelings—that I'm undeserving, that I'm shameful, that I'm wretched and unworthy—rise up like a volcano whenever I'm with her," he told me.

Then he experienced one of those moments when the truth becomes clear, when the clouds move away and the sun illuminates everything. He recognized he was perpetuating the old pain from his childhood in his present relationship with this woman. He was reliving a pattern.

The reason? It was a familiar feeling. Imagine how it feels when you scratch poison ivy. He was satisfying the itch but making the rash worse. And as long as he kept scratching, his pain would never heal.

I understood where my friend was coming from. I'd been there. But with God's guidance, I was given the gift of grace to break through a similar upbringing and rise above. As Psalms 16:11 (NASB) says:

> *You will make known to me the path of life; In Your presence is fullness of joy; In Your right hand there are pleasures forever.*

My friend had yet to have his own experience with the Lord's teaching. But at least now his mind made the connection on an emotional and psychological level. He knew he was imprisoned in a toxic relationship. He recognized the way this partner kept him trapped in depression and defeat. He understood that he'd allowed his girlfriend to become a surrogate for his family members who'd disrespected him in similar ways.

He also realized that he needed to make a clean break.

Once he made these connections, he decided to leave his relationship and put some distance between himself and his family members.

And there's more happy news. He soon got into a new relationship with a beautiful woman. Because he was able to recognize the source of his pain and no longer felt the need to relive it, he was able to open his heart and fall in love with a soul who offered him kindness and understanding—something we all deserve.

+ Can you identify an old pattern that's holding you back?

31

Reacting to Damage

HAVE YOU EVER had a car accident? Man, it's upsetting. After my accident, the car was towed to a body shop where the mechanics fixed the dings and dents and repainted the area that was hit. Yet no matter how hard they tried to match the paint to the original color (and they redid it several times!), they couldn't get it quite right.

I drove my car home anyway, but each time I looked at it, I could clearly see the area where the paint was different, and it always triggered unpleasant memories of the accident. This once-fine car that used to offer me so much pleasure had now lost its value in more ways than one.

Infidelity can be a lot like a car wreck. If someone cheats on you, or you cheat on someone, try as you might to repair the damage, you probably won't be able to completely escape reminders. You can stay together and work on it, attempt to repair your connection, and even forgive, but it's likely each time you take a hard look, you'll be reminded of the betrayal. The relationship, once so shiny and new, will have lost some value. Distrust, like car rust, can lead to continuing and even permanent erosion.

Understanding this truth, I wrote my movie *Temptation*. It's about a married woman—a marriage counselor—who is seduced by a handsome, wildly rich, charismatic entrepreneur. The movie portrays the power of temptation and the ways infidelity can lead down a disastrous path. In my film, the marriage counselor reveals her tragic story to a client to try to prevent her from making the same mistakes. The counselor lost a loving husband and her self-respect because of the affair. Although she found another way to live, the cost was great.

Not all infidelity ends as tragically as the one portrayed in *Temptation*. Couples can stay together, but they need to be honest and ask themselves, "What is my heart telling me? Does my heart still want to be in this relationship? Can I get to a place where I can trust again? Can I feel comfortable enough to accept that my partner is being wholly honest and faithful? Do I still want to travel through life beside this person?"

Whatever the scenario, whether the relationship ends or continues, there's damage—visible or invisible. Just like my car after the accident, it may still be able to get you from here to there, but the ride may never be the same again.

• Have you ever led two lives at one time? What were the consequences for you and for the people who were close to you? What lessons have you learned from the experience?

• If you were the person being deceived, can you forgive? What have you learned?

32

Reading My Book of Revelation

A BOUT TEN YEARS ago I started to keep a journal to remind myself of all the miracles I've seen in my life. There's not a day that goes by I don't say, "Thank you, Jesus. This is an amazing ride." Whether my heart is open and flowing with love and compassion, or I'm feeling stuck or hurt, if there's time, I'll reach for my journal, open to a blank page, and let the words pour out.

But lately I've been so crazy busy, the only chance to catch up on my journal writing is while I'm flying. If it's a smooth ride, I'll find peace in the air. No one is interrupting me, so I can tune in to the steady stream of my thoughts. But on my last flight to the West Coast, I opened my journal and instead of writing, I used the quiet airtime to read through it—more than one hundred pages of raw truth. I'll admit, some of it—especially the earlier entries—I found pretty disturbing.

Page by page, my life's negative force revealed itself through my own words. I saw that in the past I had been taking one step forward and four steps back. I was sabotaging myself. It was all old stuff. As a child, I was told I didn't deserve happiness. I didn't deserve success. As long as those words still lived inside me, as long as I fed them with the energy of resentment, I felt unworthy and angry.

How did I overcome my sense of unworthiness and heal? Forgiveness.

It took years and tears, and plenty of pages of ranting, but eventually I managed to forgive everyone who had hurt me in my past. My life became balanced, and I could move higher without falling back.

It's similar to the way an airplane works. On airplanes there's something called the center of gravity, or CG. All the weight from passengers, fuel, luggage, and so forth has to be balanced, or the CG won't be right and the plane will not be able to get off the ground. Well, it's the same for us. Without forgiveness, there's nothing to balance the hurt and anger. You can't reach higher, and you won't be able to make a smooth landing.

If you're going to be truly successful in what you're doing, or trying to do, you have to balance your soul or there's no takeoff. You'll expend too much energy in a downward direction. If Jesus can forgive us for our sins, surely we can step up and forgive those who have hurt us.

But, okay, let's admit it—that's no easy task. As I've learned in my life, forgiveness doesn't happen overnight. It takes time and commitment and a genuine desire to live without anger and bitterness. A good first step to getting to this peaceful place is to write down your hurt. Let it all out. *All of it.*

Once you're through writing it down, ask God for help.

You want the path to forgiveness to be cleared. You want to let go of the mind loop of blame. You want to let go of the fire of anger. You want to stop tasting the bitterness of betrayal and hurt.

Once your path is cleared . . . the sky is the limit.

• Consider Matthew 5:23–24 (ESV):
So if you are offering your gift at the altar and there remember that your brother has something against you, leave your gift there before the altar and go. First be reconciled to your brother, and then come and offer your gift.

• Write a letter to the person who hurt you. In it, express how you felt in the past and how you're trying to forgive and heal. If it's authentic, wish this person well. (You don't need to send the letter.)

PART FOUR

Harvesting the Fruit

BY UNDERSTANDING AND LEARNING FROM past and present experiences in my life, and using my expanded awareness and strong faith, I'm ready to harvest the fruit of my heartfelt labors. Every day, I feel enormous gratitude to God and to everyone and everything in my life that has brought me to this point. I'm also ready in any given moment to reach higher.

My hope is that you've also opened your soul and have found the inspiration to know it's your time to reap the sweet fruit. If you've gained an ability to envision a new level, nourish your faith, and embrace humility along the way; if you have a yearning to reach, and an understanding that sometimes you need to stand; if you've gained trust that a closed door is only a message to move on; if you have the fortitude to keep moving and to go deeper, and have embraced a willingness and desire to help others, you're making the climb.

If you've developed an understanding and appreciation for all the people who have been here to guide you—whether it's been through love or pain or forgiveness—you're ready for higher.

Everything has worked in God's perfect way to bring you to this very precious moment of higher. You're ready for your dream to manifest.

33

Giving Back

WHILE I WAS working on the play *A Madea Christmas* I heard the song "Mary, Did You Know?" playing over the audio system. My mother was the inspiration for all my Madea stories, and this one was no exception. I'd heard this song several times before, but in this particular moment the lyrics struck a resonant chord that touched my soul. I stopped what I was doing and gave my full attention to the lyrics:

> Did you know that your baby boy
> has come to make you new?
> This child that you've delivered,
> will soon deliver you?

My mother had recently died, and I had been thinking about her, as I so often did. I realized those lyrics pretty much described our situation perfectly.

> Maxine, did you know
> that your baby boy

would grow up to do
all the things he'd promised you?

Believe me, I'm certainly not comparing myself to Christ. Yet, in mortal and material ways, I was given the grace to be able to take care of my mother in her later years. As I explained previously, I made a vow as a young boy: "One day I'm going to give Mamma all she needs and deserves." Thanks to the blessings of grace, I was able to keep my vow.

I remember a particularly emotional phone conversation during my mother's final years on earth. She was sobbing, and I tried my best to calm her down. Truthfully, my heart was clenched in fear—I was worried there was some terrible piece of news about her health that she was about to share. But no, that wasn't it. Her tears were an expression of love; they were an acknowledgment.

"I just wanted to thank you, son, because if it weren't for you, I wouldn't be here," she wept. "I wouldn't be able to afford my medicine."

My mother was seriously ill, and her medicine at the time cost four or five times more than her $600 monthly Social Security check. I don't know what she would have done if I weren't able to step up and pay for it.

Mary, did you know . . .
This child that you've delivered,
will soon deliver you?

Such a powerful question. The very child that God has put in your house, whom you took care of in your youth, may be the child who cares for you as you age.

With the gifts God gave me, I could take my mother out of poverty, deliver her to a life she'd only dreamed of, and offer her the hope and care she so profoundly deserved.

I understood my mother's poignant thank-you. We had been through tough, harrowing times together. Because I had reached higher, I was able to deliver. And I knew whom to thank in return. As James 1:17 (NKJV*) reminds us,

Every good gift and every perfect gift is from above, and comes down from the Father of lights.

- Are you caring for a parent now and feeling stressed or overwhelmed? Consider this affirmation: "When I feel that I am carrying too much on my shoulders, I am reminded that I am not

---

*   New King James Version

doing it alone. God is with me. I comfort others and am comforted in return."

• Here's a good entry for your gratitude journal: Acknowledge the sacrifices (big or small) that your parents made for you and express your gratitude.

34

Embracing Life

RECENTLY A REPORTER asked me, "When you were growing up in New Orleans, did you ever imagine you would be in *this* position?"

Without hesitation I simply said, "Yes, I did."

The reporter's eyes widened. He seemed surprised and responded with a slight smirk, "Isn't that a little arrogant?"

Since he was shooting me a look of disbelief I figured he wasn't going to print what I had to say (because usually when you talk about God, reporters think it's not "publishable"), but I went on to share my view anyway.

"The truth is I *had* to imagine myself in a better place," I explained. "Because sometimes the nights got so cold and the days so hard, if I didn't dream of better times, I wouldn't have made it."

Then I shared a favorite scripture, one that has guided me through life: *The power of life and death lie in the tongue.*

"You can speak life or you can speak death," I went on. "I chose to speak life into my situation. I chose to use my imagination to take me higher. Not just in this life, but higher in Christ."

The reporter probably didn't believe me. He might not have understood what I meant, or he might have thought my words weren't appropriate for his readership—that's not what matters. I want *you* to take my message into your heart: If God can bring me out of poverty and despair and place me right in the middle of the life I'd always imagined, he can do the same for anyone. And that includes you.

The conviction that you can change your life starts with your own thinking. If you're going through dark times and it feels as if there's not enough breath and light in your soul to keep you moving higher, you need to believe that *now* is the time to break through. The seed of change starts as a thought in your own mind. You begin by believing it.

My prayer is that you begin to live in the place that God has prepared for you. Use the glorious tool of your imagination to lead you there. Envision doing better, and it shall come to pass. It has no choice. Remember Proverbs 23:7 (KJV): *For as he thinketh in his heart, so is he.*

In other words, what you think of you and hold in your heart becomes who you are.

• When you think of tomorrow, do you imagine good things are waiting for you? If not, practice switching your mindset so

you imagine a place filled with beauty
and possibility.

• Describe your more beautiful world. Let
your imagination run wild with positivity.

35

Paying Attention

I'M A NATURE lover and, as you probably know by now, I have a particular fondness for trees and plants. That said, I wouldn't say I was born with a green thumb. But over the years, and because of both successful and not-so-successful experiences, I've learned to tend to my plants by giving them individual attention and care. For example, when I'm going out of town for a while, I'll move some pots closer to the windows, set the room temperature to the desired level, and arrange for someone to water each plant according to its needs. The best way to know what a plant needs is to test its soil.

But it's not just about the water, sunlight, and temperature. Some plants take up a lot of room and require large pots, while others remain small and exist comfortably in tiny containers. Some outgrow their pots and need to be replanted frequently, while others take longer to grow. Whether it's a delicate bonsai, a sturdy succulent on the table, or a big ficus tree in the corner, all plants need the same thing—attention.

Often when I'm evaluating relationships in my life, I think about those plants—the individual care required in order for each to survive and grow. This connection has helped me offer to family and friends the particular assistance they need to thrive. It helps me tend to their specific needs. That said, all relationships, no matter how intimate or how casual, need a certain amount of nourishment, care, and attention.

And we're no exception. We need to check in with ourselves, too. Sometimes we outgrow the pots holding us. That's why it's important to look both outside and within and note if we're being limited by our surroundings. I'm not talking about the size of your living space; I mean the vision we create for ourselves.

Is it time for you to be transferred to a bigger pot?

If you're not growing anymore, if it feels as if the walls are closing in on you, if your roots are pressing up against one another and it's uncomfortable, if you're not getting enough spiritual nourishment and encouragement, then it's probably time to move to a bigger pot—a larger world.

It might mean you're ready for a leap in grace. It could be time to let more people into your life, the kind who can help you elevate. Maybe you're ready to change your approach to challenges.

Remember we are all evolving souls.

Sometimes we need to supply ourselves with the permission, nourishment, and attention to grow even greater.

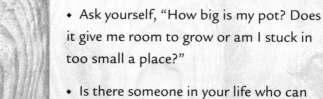

• Ask yourself, "How big is my pot? Does it give me room to grow or am I stuck in too small a place?"

• Is there someone in your life who can use your attention?

• Take a quiet walk in nature and spend time with the trees and plants. What messages are they offering you?

36

Picturing No Regrets

M Y MOTHER PASSED away on December 8, 2009. A year later, almost to the day, I was looking through a photo album and came across pictures of Mamma during her last months on earth. One in particular drew me in, and I allowed the memories it evoked to hold me close.

In this photograph, Maxine had just come home after a long afternoon of dialysis treatment. She was clearly exhausted, but I could also see she was beaming with happiness, radiating a smile as bright as the sun. In the picture, we're stepping carefully up the driveway to her house. I remember clearly she was having a tough time walking the short distance to the door. Her breath was labored, and she leaned her weakened frame against my arm. Yet, despite the physical difficulty, she was still so joyful. She was telling me how much she loved her home—how thankful she was for it.

"I would never imagine being able to live in such a fine house," she told me. "I always wanted to know what it was like to live like Mrs. Chancellor." (That's a character from Mamma's favorite soap opera, *The Young and the Restless*.)

And she added, with a voice as smooth as silk, "I wondered what it was like to have a maid—and now I *know!*"

We laughed together for a while, and once we were done being silly, I asked her, "Well, Mamma, how *does* having this make you feel?"

My mother stopped walking, stood in her tracks, and looked straight up and into my eyes. *"Loved,"* she said, tenderly squeezing my arm and managing an even bigger smile.

When the memory of that afternoon loosened its grip on me, I glanced at the bottom of the photograph and read the date it was taken: *January 4, 2009.* Within the year, Mamma would be gone. Suddenly shaken by the way time moves, I asked myself, "Do I have any regrets?" I allowed the question to settle in my soul and gave it real consideration. The answer came back loud and clear: "I have no regrets." And with that answer a great wave of peace washed over me.

Through grace, I was able to give my mother every dream she ever imagined: She owned a home that had existed only in her fantasies; she saw the ocean for the first time in her life when she came out to the West Coast to visit me; she said she'd always wanted to go on a cruise, and I took her on one. All of those things are great, but when I say I have no regrets, I mean I did everything I could to make sure her life was full and abundant with love and care.

I aimed for my love to be a constant in her life, from our almost-daily phone calls and coming home every chance I got (despite having to see Emmitt there for many years), to giving her hugs and sitting with her during dialysis treatments. I let her know I was there in the truest sense.

I have no regrets because I made her proud. I made her feel strong even when she was physically weak by becoming the person she raised—a kind, compassionate, and loving soul. I wanted to be that kid for her, and I was willing to go wherever it took me. I kept my vow to try to do everything with honesty and fullness, in love and in kindness.

Whatever was in my heart and on my mind that we needed to talk about—we needed to share, we needed to unburden—was expressed. Nothing was left unsaid.

No regrets. That's the best feeling. I know I did everything in my power for my mother. I can say there is not one thing I would change. It's a blessing. It gives me peace at night. When I think about my mother, I don't think in terms of sorrow, sadness, or regret. Yes, I miss her, but there's no *I wish I had* . . . done this or *I wish I had* . . . done that. There are none of those moments, because I did everything I could.

Tomorrow is not promised to anyone. It's prudent for every one of us to let those people we love and care about know they're fully in our hearts. You may not be able to take care of this person financially, or be able to provide creature comforts and other stuff, but you can step up with love. Love is enough.

I keep returning to the place of love because there's nothing more valuable to give another soul. Love is fulfilling, love is all around, love grows inside of us; it's plentiful, everlasting, nourishing, bountiful, and boundless.

When people you love pass on, and they know without a shadow of a doubt that you loved them, there's not a trace of regret. You're both set free.

- If I said to you that by this time next year the person you love the most will not be here, would you have any regrets?

- What actions can you take today to let that person know they mean the world to you?

- Consider Galatians 6:2 (NIV): *Carry each other's burdens, and in this way you will fulfill the law of Christ.*

37

Finding Treasure

YOU CAN LEARN something from everything and everybody. That was certainly the case with my beloved aunt Mae. I remember how her enlightened way of being and her humble home filled my soul with both wonder and wisdom.

One of my most vivid memories is walking through the door to Mae's home and seeing an old man with skin the color of bronze lying in a narrow bed in the corner of her front room. To my little-boy eyes it looked like there were a million wrinkles running like streams down his face. His name was Papa Rod, and for a long time that was all I knew about him. Then one day Aunt Mae told me Rod had been born a slave. In those early years, I was too young for this information to hold any meaning. What really intrigued me at the time were the quilts covering Rod's rail-thin body.

The blankets were stitched together with patches from Mae's worn-out dresses and scraps of rags. In my immaturity, I thought those old quilts looked really ugly. "What the heck are those raggedy things doing covering that poor old man?" I'd think. "Why doesn't Mae go to a store like Kent's or TG&Y and get good blankets like the ones Mamma has?"

But there was no getting away from those "ugly" old quilts. At night, when it was time for me to be tucked into bed, Mae would bring a few of her hand-stitched treasures and pile them on top of me. I can still feel the weight of those old blankets pressing against my stomach and the smell of mothballs wafting up to my nostrils. But, ugly though they were, those quilts sure kept me warm.

Years later, when I was twenty, I moved from my home in New Orleans to Atlanta. As one of my goodbye gifts, my mother handed me a quilt. By then, I was mature enough to recognize all the hard work that went into making the blanket. So I appreciated it, but honestly? It still embarrassed me a little.

Shortly after I moved to Atlanta, life got really tough. I was living in a small one-bedroom basement apartment and paying $340 a month in rent. But even that was too much because I was putting all my money into producing my plays, and I fell behind on the rent. One afternoon I drove up to the apartment building and saw all my stuff thrown out on the street. I was in total shock. To make matters worse, it was raining. I got out of my car and tried to gather anything of value that was still left for the grabbing. My neighbors had already picked through much of it, but right there in front of me, on the ground, drenched and worn-out, was Aunt Mae's quilt. I piled as many clothes as I could on top of the patchwork blanket, then rolled it up. Defeated and depressed, I threw the wet heap into the trunk of my car and drove off. Those few possessions went into storage while I tried to find a place to live. Sadly, a few months later, I couldn't even afford to pay the storage bill and lost everything, including the quilt.

Years later, when my life turned around, I glanced in the window of an upscale New Orleans antiques store, and center stage was a quilt that looked very much like one of Mae's. Instantly I felt a rush of memories. I knew it couldn't be the same one, but I also knew that someone's grandmother or great-aunt had sewn that quilt out of old dresses and rags. Suddenly, the scorching heat of shame spread through me. I hadn't taken such good care of the one that was given to me. As I studied the lines and stitching, I got a lump in my throat. What my young eyes once saw as ugly, I could now see was truly a masterpiece.

I went into the store and inquired about the quilt. The shopkeeper was more than happy to share its history, explaining it was made by an African American woman and had been carefully preserved over the years by her family. All the fabrics dated back to different times in history. The patches ranged in age from the Civil War to the civil rights movement. I asked how much the quilt was worth.

"These kinds of rare quilts, with their deep history and fine handiwork, sell for between $12,000 and $100,000," she told me.

My jaw hit the floor. I was embarrassed that I'd had this kind of sentimental and material treasure in my house, in my possession, in my life, and I had treated it carelessly, as if it were a rag.

With a bit of distance, it occurred to me that the quilt acted as a metaphor for our human condition. Sometimes there are people in our lives who should be treated like treasures and instead we treat them like rags. We may even discard them. We use them only when we need to be warm or comforted. Like that quilt, we think they're worthless, and it may take somebody else to point out their value to us; unfortunately, it may be long after the person has left our lives.

The flip side can also be true. You may be like that quilt, allowing yourself to be treated as if you don't matter, or being pushed aside or used only when you are needed. Realize you are worth more than those people know. Like that quilt, you are beautiful. It takes all those patches of your personal history to make you whole and who you are.

And, like the quilt, if you give warmth to people and they don't return your offering, understand that you have value beyond what they recognize. You are made from fabric that has endured, seen more than many people can imagine—and you're still here, still offering warmth. If someone is too blind or unsophisticated to appreciate your beauty, another soul who has lived a deep life and has developed maturity will recognize your worth. Just like that quilt, you are a treasure; your story matters. And you should be cherished.

I wish Aunt Mae's quilt would have come with a label saying VALUE ME NOW AND VALUE ME IN THE FUTURE. If so, maybe when I was a young and foolish man I would have known the treasure I possessed.

But all was not lost.

Thank God, I was able to grab the unforgettable lesson from this experience, hold it close, and have it keep me warm and offer comfort for the rest of my life.

• Is there someone you are taking for granted? In what ways are they a true treasure? What can you do to show your appreciation?

• On the other hand, is someone taking you for granted?

• Imagine the events of your life as individual patches. Draw a picture of your life's quilt and label each powerful event.

38

Cherishing the True Gift

WHEN DID I first consider myself successful?
Around the time my first play started touring and
I was able to support my mother financially. I thought it was
time for her to retire from her job at the Jewish community
center where she had worked for years as a teacher's assis-
tant. She loved the children, but it was terribly exhausting,
especially after she became ill. When she was finally able to
rely completely on me, I felt I'd made it in a way that really
counted.

Around the same time I was able to start carrying her
burden, Christmas presents from Mamma to me became an
ongoing problem. My mother loved Christmas and loved
giving gifts, and she'd bring it up during our telephone
conversations—*a lot*.

"Junior, you're so hard to shop for," she would say. "I just
don't know what to get you for Christmas."

"No, no . . . you know, Mamma, I have everything I need."

But she insisted. "Yeah, I know you have everything you
need and everything you want—that's the problem!"

"You can, too! Anything you want, Mamma, I can make sure you have it!" That response would get us laughing like two kids over a school joke. Of course, I was serious. . . . I would have given Maxine anything.

But I understood. She really wanted to buy me a Christmas present. The holidays meant a lot to her, and not knowing what gift to get me was driving her crazy.

The next time we were together at Thanksgiving, I gave her my answer. "Mamma," I said. "You know what? I'd really love a pair of flannel pajamas." She looked back at me as happy as one of Santa's elves, eyes bright with delight. Problem solved.

Every Christmas, for the next four years, she would go to Walmart and buy me a pair of plaid flannel pajamas. And every Christmas when the family was gathered together at her house I'd see the gift under the tree, pretend to be surprised, and smile inside and out. "Exactly what I wanted!" I'd bellow with full-blast enthusiasm.

Just to give you a quick peek at my mother's priorities, she didn't put a lot of appreciation or energy into wrapping gifts. That wasn't her style. When I was a kid, she wouldn't wrap a thing. Christmas mornings the family would walk into the living room and our unwrapped toys would be laid out under the tree. Mamma would say, "That's for you . . . and that's for you . . . and that's for you," pointing to the gifts and their recipients.

Her philosophy? "I ain't wasting no damn money on wrapping paper!"

Back to the pajamas. Needless to say, over the years I collected a nice pile of PJs that were in all ways too small.

The tops were so short the sleeves were almost to my elbows, and the bottoms were several inches above my ankles.

One morning, a few years after my mother died, I was getting ready for work at the studio and looking for something. I've forgotten what it was, but the search led me to open a drawer in my closet where I kept all those ill-fitting pajamas. When I found them my heart flew open as if it were a bird suddenly taking flight. It released the memories of Christmas mornings right from my soul and reminded me of my mother and how all she'd wanted to do was give. I also remembered how Christmas was one of the few times in our family's life when we were at peace under one roof.

Later that night, when I came home, I actually put on a pair of those flannel pajamas and wore them to bed. Short sleeves, high waist—I didn't care. Those PJs reminded me of my mother's soul and made me warm and happy.

Those pajamas were among the most precious gifts I've ever received because they came from my mother's heart. A gift that comes from the heart is more valuable than the most expensive present in the world. And though this might sound like a cliché, the biggest, the best, gift is love. When you feel true love, when you know love, you've been given *everything*. It's not the pajamas per se; they didn't matter. What my mother was giving me was the reminder of how much she loved me.

Opening that drawer and seeing those pajamas made me feel that love all over again, even though she has passed on. It was like a soothing balm. When I wore those flannel PJs, I experienced the warmth of her hug. It was amazing.

It doesn't really matter what gift you give someone, or whether it has fancy bows, satiny ribbons, or flashy paper around it; when it's wrapped in love, it's the best—the most valuable—present you can give someone.

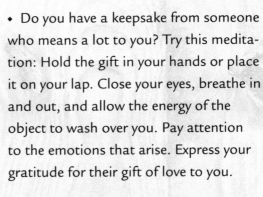

• Do you have a keepsake from someone who means a lot to you? Try this meditation: Hold the gift in your hands or place it on your lap. Close your eyes, breathe in and out, and allow the energy of the object to wash over you. Pay attention to the emotions that arise. Express your gratitude for their gift of love to you.

• Consider this verse from 1 Corinthians 12:4 (ESV): *Now there are varieties of gifts, but the same Spirit.*

39

Seeding for Growth

WHEN YOU PLANT a seed a few inches deep in the earth, you can't see it, but it doesn't mean the seed is not growing. Know this: As long as you tend to it with positive energy, an unseen dynamic will take place, pushing it in the direction of growth. You may not see the progress right away. For that, you need faith.

I've already written a bit about my first play, *I Know I've Been Changed*. It was such a powerful force in my life. It taught me that we don't always see our life changing shape while it's happening.

Trying to get my play off the ground required a leap of faith. Imagine jumping from the peak of one mountain to the next with only trust in God giving you the courage to do it. I invested and invested and invested—putting every cent I had and every ounce of energy into the show. I was also working with a promoter who was putting money into the project. Some nights, once the curtain went down, we'd count ticket sales and discover that we hadn't made a dime. The promoter would shrug his shoulders with a hint of defeat. "Hey, I didn't make any money tonight," he would complain.

And during those times, I would reply, "Don't pay me. Keep that money and put it back into the show. We've got to get this play off the ground!"

There were no hard facts to back it up, but I had a strong feeling that a seed of success was germinating underground. I had faith. We weren't seeing the results moment to moment, but an energy was mounting. I had faith. It was growing.

In the beginning of the run, the crowds weren't there, but I kept sowing and sowing—and believing. I had faith. Seven years later, the seed burst from the ground and blossomed. *I Know I've Been Changed* was a hit, like a flower shooting up from the earth. I finally experienced the sweet smell of success. Faith had kept me going. It turned my life around.

You also have to understand that only God can give the increase. You can plant one million seeds, water them, fertilize them, and take every precaution, but if God doesn't give the increase, you won't be able to make that seed grow. What I've learned is this: Do all you can do; pray for the rest—and keep the faith.

When I was taking *I Know I've Been Changed* on the road, I was nurturing an audience a little bit at a time. Just growing it, just tilling the soil and helping people who came to the show to enjoy themselves, feel happiness, have a good time, and associate fun with my name.

There's an old adage: "Let nature take its course." Now, that's true, but you also need the combination of toil and faith—and that includes hard work, prayer, and *surrender.* You can't be too hooked on the outcome. Full faith, full prayer, is truly about surrender. When Jesus was praying in Gethsemane, he said, *"Let this bitter cup pass from me."* He said that because it was so difficult, maybe he thought he couldn't get through it—and then he surrendered: *"Nevertheless, let not my will but Your will be done."*

In asking that God's will be done, we can nevertheless pray for many things, and I prayed for many things over the years. Some manifested, others didn't. I'm as grateful for those that didn't come to fruition as for those that grew and ripened. The ones that didn't make it weren't in the will of God. My life would have taken a different course, and I'm filled with gratitude for the way my life has grown.

It's this simple: Prayer is the seed. Faith is the watering. Hard work is the sun delivering the nutrients the seed needs to grow. It gives it the force to break through. James 2:14 (NET Bible) says,

> *What good is it, my brothers and sisters, if someone claims to have faith but does not have works?*

Faith without hard works is dead. You can't sit around saying to yourself, "I want to get rich," or "I want my business to be successful," or "I want my family to feel loving," and then do nothing about it.

There's another element to add to the formula. Make sure the nutrients you deliver through hard work are filled with light. If you think you can take a shortcut by doing something that is unkind or even illegal, you won't be on the side of God. And without His help, whatever grows won't give you deep joy. What would be the point?

Joy, love, satisfaction, gratitude, and the ability to give to others—that's what a successful life is about.

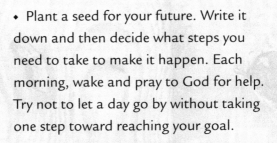

• Plant a seed for your future. Write it down and then decide what steps you need to take to make it happen. Each morning, wake and pray to God for help. Try not to let a day go by without taking one step toward reaching your goal.

• Consider Galatians 6:9 (ESV): *And let us not grow weary of doing good, for in due season we will reap, if we do not give up.*

40

Digging Deeper

I USED TO GET these outrageously high water bills. I knew it wasn't because I was taking five-hour showers. What was drinking up all the water? It had to be the lawn. I have sprinklers going all the time in the summer to prevent the grass from drying out. The lawn needed water to live and thrive—so what, I wondered, could I do to keep the water bills down? It took me a little while, but I figured it out: I'd hire a company to dig a well on my property. That way I wouldn't have to use the municipal water supply with its crazy bills. My lawn and I would be self-sufficient.

A few days later, I'm walking on my lawn, talking to the foreman of a respected engineering company. As we're busy shooting the breeze, he's sticking orange flags attached to skinny sticks into the ground.

"What are those for?" I asked.

"These might be good places to dig for water," he told me.

"Well, why are there so many?"

"I'm just not sure if any of these places will produce water," he said in a flat voice, as a simple matter of fact.

Flabbergasted, I said, *"If?* Hold up! You mean if you dig *all* these spots and don't find water, I still have to pay you?"

"That's how it goes," was the foreman's answer.

Well, he'd been in the business for quite a while so I figured he knew what he was doing. What else could I say? Reluctantly, I agreed to this plan. But the next week, after the company had dug three deep holes with their fancy equipment and didn't find a drop of water, I became frustrated and gave the order to stop.

Months went by and the insane water bills kept coming. Finally, I relented. I called the engineering company back and said, "Keep digging until you hit water."

When the workers returned, they drilled down five hundred feet with no success.

"Do you want us to stop?" the foreman asked.

This time I didn't hesitate.

"Go deeper," I said.

They dug another two hundred feet and still—nothing.

"Go deeper."

They drilled another 200 feet. *Nothing.*

"Blast it, cut it, do whatever you have to do, but keep digging until you find water!" I said.

After fighting the rocks, breaking their drill, bringing in a new one, and resuming the dig, the foreman told me, "Well, we're at twelve hundred feet—do you want me to keep going?"

I said, "Keep going. I'm sick of those water bills."

But he warned me: "We usually never have to go down *this* deep, and we haven't hit water yet. It's already going to be very expensive."

I thought for a moment but held my resolve. "Sometimes you have to go deeper to get what you're after, no matter what the cost."

Once more the workers fired up the big noisy machine and drilled down further. This time after digging only *four* inches more—*Eureka!* The water gushed up like a geyser! Imagine that: We had been just four inches away from the big breakthrough.

It's now years later, and the well has not run dry. I never got another whopping water bill, either.

Has something similar ever happened to you? Have you spent a lot of time on something even if it seems like you're getting nowhere? Well, if you're sure your focus is where you want it to be—and where God wants it to be—keep digging deeper. Don't stop praying until you live the change you've been waiting for. Don't stop exploring, and pushing, and focusing, until you deliver the breakthrough.

You might hit rock. There will probably be costs, some of them unexpected. But once you get to where God wants you to be, you'll get it all back and more.

As 1 Samuel 30:8 (KJV)—one of my favorite scriptures—says,

Pursue: for thou shalt surely overtake them and without fail recover all.

Don't give up digging. You might be mere inches away.

• Fear of failure or feelings of frustration can hold us back and keep us from giving our all to a venture. When have you over-come one of these emotional obstacles? What happened?

41

Writing to a Friend

I WROTE A LETTER to a friend whose father has never been there for him. Even though my friend is not a kid anymore—he's a husband and father himself—it was obvious to me that he was still being affected negatively by his past. There was an emotional wall preventing him from moving on. I wanted to help.

This is what I wrote:

Hey, Bud,

Your dad is getting older and facing his mortality. He's going to become a different man soon. In life, we all become different people. At fifty, you're not the same person you were at twenty. We are built to evolve. Life is an oven that incubates us into change—most times for the better.

My challenge to you, my friend, is to start looking at your father like an individual. He has his own soul, his own history, his own trials and tribulations. Don't look at the man you see now, but the boy he once was. Envision how he grew up, and imagine what he went through.

Realize that just like you he's had pain, heartbreak, struggles, secrets, disappointments, and sadness. In other words, he had a life and a complicated story long before you were born. In that life he wasn't prepared properly to be the father you needed him to be.

It's like this: When you go on a trip, you pack a suitcase and fill it with everything you'll need. A parent's job is to help their child pack a suitcase for the journey of life. It should be packed with confidence, patience, joy, and hope. It needs to be filled with lessons on how to accept and share heart, how to have faith in God, and how to feel His grace. All these things and much more should be packed into the suitcase. If they aren't, that child is going to have a tough life.

Consider, my friend, what's in your father's suitcase. It's probably missing some essentials. That's not an excuse for the way he treats you, but it can help you to understand him. I know he's shut down. I know you don't know much about his history. If he won't tell you more, then maybe one of his family members will share his story. His past is important in helping you to comprehend your present. Do you understand?

At any rate, I don't care who or what he is. I'm just glad he was used by God to bring such an awesome soul like you into this world. Whether he will ever know it or not, I thank him for that. I thank him for you.

I love you, my friend.

My friend phoned me in tears right after he read the letter. "Tyler, I don't know how to thank you for this," he said.

"All I know is that I'm going to take in all this wisdom, and whether my father accepts me or not, and is part of my life or not, I have a better understanding now of what his journey may have been. I can start on a path to forgiveness and hope to move on from there."

My intention was to open my friend's heart and mind about his father's experience. And I could tell by our conversation that he got it. I think in the long run, this understanding—and his offer of forgiveness—will also help him to be a better, more open and loving father to his two beautiful girls. When parents are good and loving, God-fearing and full-of-soul people, their children become their healers.

It becomes a circle of love.

• Have you forgiven *your* parents for their shortcomings? Can you switch the focus from blaming them to understanding yourself? Can you offer them forgiveness?

42

Looking Ahead

PICTURE THIS: You get into the front seat of your new, perfect car, turn your body around, and put your knees on the front seat and your back against the steering wheel. You're not facing the dashboard but, rather, are turned around in your seat, facing the trunk. You stay in this awkward position while trying to drive. If by some miracle (and it would be a miracle) you manage to move forward, I guarantee you won't go far. It would be nearly impossible!

Imagine the car is your life, and you're not getting anywhere. What if there's nothing wrong with the car, but you're just sitting in it backward? What if there's nothing really wrong with your life, you're just facing the wrong direction?

There are many things that cause you to be out of alignment with life, but a really common one that keeps us facing backward is *guilt*.

I once had a conversation with a friend who was telling me about all the things he feels guilty about: His marriage fell apart, he doesn't get to see his kids very often, he's not in a financial position to do more for them, he's wasted so much money, he's wasted so much time . . . guilt, guilt, guilt. Finally I had to say, "Enough!"

Once he calmed down, I reminded him of a few things.

Guilt can destroy us. We all make mistakes. We've all fallen short. At some point, we've all disappointed someone, especially ourselves. Unfortunately, there's nothing you can do about it. These events have already happened; they're in the past. Instead of facing backward, beating yourself up, how about putting your energy into making sure it doesn't happen again? How about facing forward? And while you're at it, how about helping to heal anyone you may have hurt while you were turned in the wrong direction?

If you allow guilt to consume you, it will win. You can't let guilt take over your thoughts. If you do, you'll enter into a downward spiral that will keep you looking in the wrong direction. Guilt is an emotion that makes you feel unworthy, and when you feel unworthy, you don't believe in yourself. You think you don't deserve good things in your life. When that's your view, you're not able to move in the right direction. You make wrong turns and get lost again and again. And then what's likely to happen? More guilt. Do you see the cycle? Guilt trips are a ride to nowhere.

In order to set yourself free, you have to let go of guilt, or it will bind and grind you. How do you say "So long" to guilt? This may surprise you, but it's a process of forgiveness.

The first book of John, 1:9 (ESV), says:

If we confess our sins, he is faithful and just to forgive us our sins and to cleanse us from all unrighteousness.

Begin by asking for forgiveness from anyone you've hurt. Ask God for His forgiveness. And, most of all, ask yourself for forgiveness. Don't face the wrong way. You can't get to the great things ahead if you're always looking backward.

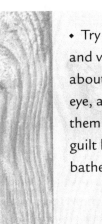

• Try this meditation: Sit in a quiet place and visualize the person you feel guilty about. Once this person is in your mind's eye, ask for their forgiveness. Next, see them forgiving you. Feel the weight of guilt lifting, and imagine you're both bathed in light.

43

Belonging in the Room

I N 2005, I received an invitation to Oprah's Legends Ball.
My first movie had just premiered, *Diary of a Mad Black
Woman,* and the play that launched my career, *I Know I've
Been Changed,* had been doing well for a few years. Despite
these successes, my deeper self-judgment told me, "Tyler,
you're not good enough to be with these amazing people."
That said, I wouldn't have missed it for the world. With ex-
citement and some trepidation, I RSVP'd "Yes!"

A few months later, I found myself strolling the luxuri-
ous grounds of Bacara Resort in Goleta, California, where
the event was held. The sun was glistening on three swim-
ming pools, and shining down on massive clay tennis courts,
an eighteen-hole golf course, and an endless stretch of
beachfront. Just as I was thinking to myself that the word
"grand" seemed an understatement, a long, lanky man
sprinted by, drenched in perspiration. I realized it was Sena-
tor Barack Obama (he wasn't president yet), and as he
passed by like a breeze, I felt the touch of his grace, ease,
and confidence.

Later in the day, I put on what turned out to be a pretty ill-fitting suit. The jacket was way too long, and when I checked myself out in the mirror, I remember thinking it looked like I was wearing a zoot suit. But time was moving on and I had to get to the event. I made my anxious walk to the ballroom.

At the entrance I stopped in my tracks and scanned the room. There were so many beautiful human beings there, people I'd deeply admired for years, souls I'd idolized: Coretta Scott King, Maya Angelou, Diana Ross, Katherine Dunham, John Travolta, Sidney Poitier, Cicely Tyson, Barbra Streisand, Tina Turner, Tom Cruise, Ruby Dee, Jesse Jackson, Quincy Jones, Della Reese, and Michelle Obama, among a constellation of other luminaries.

Just standing there, taking it all in, was a sort of out-of-body experience. There were flowers everywhere. Everyone was dressed in black and white except for one person, our gracious hostess, Oprah Winfrey, who was wearing a red dress.

So, there I was—standing at the entrance to the ballroom, dumbstruck by the glamour and gravity of the event and filled with *how*'s:

How did this happen?

How did I get here?

How did I go from the child struggling in New Orleans?

How did I make it from the young man living in a car and counting his pennies?

How in the world am I here?

Once my nerves settled enough to stop *how*-ing, and I could put one foot in front of the next, I crossed the threshold, walked to the long banquet table, and looked around until I found my place setting. I was seated right next to Yolanda Adams, the amazing gospel singer. With my heart blasted open and with a rush of disbelief, amazement, and gratitude, I actually said out loud, "What am I doing in this room?" I was feeling so abundant with the fullness of my life, I guess I couldn't contain myself.

Yolanda turned to me, looked me right in the eye, and said, "Tyler, you belong in the room. We all belong here."

Those words were powerful. I breathed deeply and needed a few moments in silence to allow her message to sink in. Yolanda centered me and figuratively pulled my feet down into the room with that statement: "You belong here." It was a tremendous gift and blessing, because it helped me take the fullness of the experience in. Once I was grounded, everything around me looked so much more vibrant—the flowers, the crystals in the chandelier, and all the remarkable guests.

In that clear-as-glass moment, I got it.

God had placed me in this room.

Once we were all seated, playwright and poet Pearl Cleage recited her poem "We Speak Your Names." At the end of her invocation, these amazing women stood up to proclaim and speak the names of the legends that were being honored. To hear those names called and see the expressions of love and caring from Oprah to these women, and the tears in everyone's eyes—this was truly a shining, unforgettable moment in my life and one that gave me this guidance:

When God puts you somewhere, you need to not only appreciate it, but also understand that even though you may not feel worthy enough, there's something within you that brought God to say, *You should be here. I want to show you something.* And when this happens you have to stay open.

Pay attention.

Take it all in with gratitude.

Feel its abundance.

Explore and mine every lesson.

Release your self-judgment.

Be as aware as you can be.

I left the experience of the Legends Ball telling myself, "I'm going to dream and I'm going to dream bigger." That's how profound it was for me to know "I belong in the room."

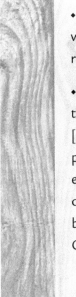

◆ Do you remember a time in your life when you felt you weren't worthy of recognition?

◆ Judgments are essentially thoughts that say, "I am [or others are] [negative quality] because of [behavior/ perceived weakness]." If you find yourself engaging in judgmental thoughts, think of ways you can release those judgments by transforming them into trust in God's judgment.

44

———

Finding Your Feet
Off the Ground

I WOKE ONE MORNING feeling unusually frustrated. No big deal, but there was so much to do to get my studio open.

My responsibilities were endless. I was just about to open my mouth and start complaining when suddenly I remembered an incident from the year before.

After a long day at work I was heading to my car when I saw a woman who appeared to be homeless walking toward me. I'm ashamed to say this, but I thought, "I don't feel like being hustled today." Then I felt an instant flash of shame and started digging in my pocket for money. As the woman got closer, I could clearly see her face and noticed that she had the kindest eyes. They were dark and tender, the color of mahogany, and despite her obvious hardship, her eyes shined with a clear light. She began to speak.

Reflexively, I thought, "Oh, no, hold on . . . here comes the sales pitch. . . ."

"Excuse me, sir," she said. "Do you have any shoes?"

Her plea sparked a memory of the time I was living out on the streets with only one pair of run-down shoes. My eyes instantly started to tear up. I was taken aback by her request and the sweet tone of her voice.

"Please come with me," I said. I put my hand on her elbow and led her inside my studio and asked the wardrobe people to find shoes in her size. They found her a perfect pair. As soon as she slipped them on her feet, she cried out, full of soul, "Praise God! Thank you, Jesus. My feet are off the ground! Lord, my feet are off the ground."

Everyone in the room had tears in their eyes, it was such an emotional moment.

All she'd wanted was shoes. That was what she needed and that was her only request. She never asked for a dime.

Once she had the shoes on her feet, she slipped out the door. It was unsettling; no one had seen her leave. Hebrews 13:2 (KJV) came to mind: *Be not forgetful to entertain strangers: for thereby some have entertained angels unawares.*

I take this to mean that you have to be careful when you're talking to someone, because that person could be an angel. And that was the message. I think everyone in the room sensed the same thing.

Holding that in my mind, I felt a yearning close to desperation to find her again. I went outside, and when I didn't see her nearby, I got in my car and started driving around asking, "God, was that an angel that came to visit us?"

And then I saw her standing on a street corner looking down at her shoes, still weeping and thanking God.

I got out of my car, walked over to her, and started a conversation.

"If I may ask, how did you become homeless?"

"I have AIDS, and my family doesn't want to have anything to do with me," she explained. "I have no place to go. Right now I'm waiting for a place in a shelter. But I know God will make a way for me."

Her faith and her praise moved me to action.

"He just did," I thought.

I took her to a nearby hotel and put her up indefinitely, with the understanding that she could stay until she could look after herself. I had one of my staff check in from time to time at the hotel to be sure she had food and clothing. After about a month or so, we lost touch. She left the hotel and disappeared again.

But I never forgot her.

The summer I was shooting *Daddy's Little Girls*, a woman walked up to me, smiling from ear to ear. I didn't recognize her right away, but her bright mahogany eyes were familiar. She was wearing a fine dress, and her hair was done up. It was *her*! The woman who'd needed shoes.

"How are you doing?" I asked, knowing by her appearance that life must have gotten a lot easier for her.

"I'm living in a nice house and doing very well," she said. "The help you offered me changed my life. I can never thank you enough."

But here's the truth: Little did this woman know that she had also given me something that changed my life, and I wanted to thank her.

After I met her, any time I think about complaining I remember her appreciation, "My feet are off the ground!" With that memory, my soul is instantly raised with the uplifting power of gratitude.

When we feel gratitude there's no room in our soul for complaints. We feel a sense of abundance. We are filled with faith, love, and confidence. We can experience the force of willingness, and our soul can surge with the zeal of higher expectations.

That's how you know your feet are off the ground.

• Remember a person who entered your life and taught you a lesson of gratitude.

• Consider 1 Thessalonians 5:18 (ESV): *Give thanks in all circumstances; for this is the will of God in Christ Jesus for you.*

45

Remembering Mamma

I OFTEN DREAM ABOUT my mother. Sometimes when I'm alone I can still hear her laughter filling the room. She had such a distinct laugh, a rapid-fire *Ha-ha-ha-ha,* one *ha* tumbling on top of the next without a breath in between. Her laughter sprang from a well of deep, authentic joy, and whenever I heard it, I knew she was truly happy, and it made me happy, too.

I can also still hear her singing in the church choir on Sunday mornings, full throttle, shouting about how good God is. In those days, I could pick out her voice from among all the other pious church ladies'. Let me tell you, it wasn't because her voice was beautiful. She had a terrible voice—completely flat and out of tune. But it didn't matter one iota. Her voice was one hundred percent rich with soul.

She would be belting out the gospel on Sunday mornings, but we never told the preacher that Mamma was singing quite a different tune on Friday and Saturday nights. Her music of choice on those evenings was the down-home blues. She'd be hanging out with our neighbors and friends who were in her card club, sipping Hennessy straight up from a Styrofoam cup and playing her hands well into the early morning. The game of choice back then was Tonk. If you know cards at all, you know it's a pretty fast game, a lot like knock rummy.

Mamma would usually get in her Cadillac and drive the ten blocks from our house on Baronne Street to the projects. Once a month it was her turn to host, and the members of the club would come to our place. Mamma was a particularly skilled card player, and she was lucky. She could make up to eleven hundred dollars from her hands, especially during the times when members were playing in our house, because the host always got a cut of the winnings.

She's still so vivid in my mind and heart. I can feel her hugging me tight, making every nerve and muscle in my body relax and feel safe, protected, and loved. When I was little, she'd hold my head into her belly, and I would get a good whiff of her Woolworth five-and-dime department store perfume and smell her cigarette smoke. "I love you, Junior," she would whisper, and that was enough for me. I knew everything was going to be all right.

When I moved out, Mamma and I still spoke nearly every day—and I would always ask if she needed anything. She would usually say the same thing: "I need you to be happy." She was big on tradition, too, and every year, no matter how old I was, she would phone and sing "Happy Birthday" to me—off-pitch, of course, but it was sweet music to my ears.

I don't know if I can truly express how proud I was of my mother, but I was. I remember her saying, "You know I did the best I could by you." And yes, I knew that. I know that she loved me like no other on this earth, and that I was her hope and dream. I still love her so much.

In the end, she couldn't go on anymore. Her body was letting her down, though I knew she wanted to stay here on earth for me. I'm glad she has no more pain. But I have pain now, missing her every single day.

It's been almost a decade since Mamma died, so it's getting easier. Knowing that she is with God helps me get through. And really, I'm okay now. I'm standing on my own, holding Mamma in my heart.

Remembering Mamma also reminds me about all those days I took for granted. I didn't cherish the finite time we had together. If you're like me, you waste too much time on things that don't really matter. Remind your soul of this truth: Our beloveds aren't promised to us forever. While you still have the chance, embrace those you love and who love you, hold them dear, tell them how much they mean to you—don't keep it to yourself. You never know when God will call them back.

♦ Consider Ephesians 4:2 (NIV):
Be completely humble and gentle; be patient, bearing with one another in love.

♦ Why not call those you love and tell them how you feel?

46

Lighting Up the World

I'VE BEEN DOING a lot of building over the past few years. I've learned that, according to the commercial codes across the country, before you can construct a building, plans must first be reviewed by a board, and they have to pass a "life safety review."

In order to pass that review, the building must meet certain requirements: It must have fire exits, sprinklers, and exit signs, as well as lights with emergency backup batteries. That means that if all the power in the building goes out, small lights that are independent of the major source of power will automatically turn on and lead the way out of darkness.

I think about those lights a lot as I look at the state of our country and the state of the world. At any given time you can turn on the news and without a doubt you'll be assaulted with darkness, negative images, death, destruction, terrorism, murder, hate, and racism. You don't have to go looking for it. These images and this information are always there, always available, as if they were meant to lead our way.

Of course, this barrage is anything but enlightening, yet it's ever-present—on our smartphones, on our laptops. When you're carrying around this kind of information on your person, it's hard not to let it seep into your heart.

If you keep taking in this negative information, it can consume you. You may become cynical, jaded, and emotionally removed from the struggles of all our brothers and sisters around the world. If you let it live in your mind and heart, you may start to think that evil is winning. It can make you feel hopeless.

While I was learning about all these horrors, I would start wondering, "Where are all the people who believe in God? Where is the good and right and just? Where are the compassionate souls who care for one another? Where are the people with the little light that my mother sang about in church? Where is the balance?"

Then I found an answer. I decided to be a balance keeper.

What do I mean by that?

When I hear about darkness, I want to do something good and kind. I couldn't stop Hurricane Katrina, but I could rebuild homes for twenty families. I couldn't stop the earthquake in Haiti, but I could donate money to help the relief effort. I couldn't save the little girls who were mauled by wild animals on their way to get fresh water in Africa, but I could help fund efforts to dig wells and bring fresh water to thousands of villagers around the world.

You see what I'm saying here? You may not have the power to stop a bomb from falling in Syria, but you can give something to a homeless shelter, if not with your money, with your time. You may not be able to stop terrorism, but you can single-handedly give bread to a hungry child.

"Well," you may say, "that's such a small gesture in the scheme of things."

Let me assure you, if all the big lights go out and it's pitch-black, and you are the only one with a tiny light, I promise we would see your little light shining, and your light could lead the way.

I challenge all of us to be balance keepers.

Light up the darkness.

Let your light shine.

• Anger and fear won't change the world for the better. What light can you shine to make a difference?

• Give yourself a break. Turn off the news for at least a few hours every day.

47

Working with Intention

A S I WAS leaving after a performance in Milwaukee's BMO Harris Bradley Center one night, we got stuck in bumper-to-bumper traffic between North Fourth and West State Street. The car was inching along at a snail's pace, about the same speed as the audience, who were exiting the arena in a thick syrupy stream. I sat behind tinted windows, watching the groups of people going by. There were smiling faces, couples strolling arm in arm or holding hands, children laughing, and groups of joyful and animated elderly folks waiting for buses. This moving tableau, full of life, energy, and jubilation, brought me right into a well of loving awareness. I was reminded of how blessed I am to be doing the work that I do.

I've been told by people that they come to see my performances to get something from me, but the truth is, they offer me so much more. Lightheartedness, glee, laughter, and hope are all contagious emotions. These cheerful, uplifting feelings unclench the heart and enrich our essence so we can be receptive to the brilliance of light and the force of positivity. My work gives me not just satisfaction, but daz-zling pleasure. Being able to do something meaningful with our lives is one of the greatest gifts we're given.

I know I'm lucky. According to a 2017 Gallup Poll, only 30 percent of folks in the United States say they are engaged in their jobs, while 70 percent say they're either "not en-gaged" or "actively disengaged" in their work. The prob-lem? The work isn't meaningful.

Maybe you harbor the desire to do a certain kind of work that you're not engaged in now. Maybe you have re-curring thoughts about something you need to accom-plish in your life. This inner voice is not arbitrary. These thoughts aren't just passing through your mind like a breeze. They're tugging at you, shaking you up for a rea-son. What's going on?

It's your destiny calling.

Truly, this is the very thing you're supposed to be doing in your life.

For whatever reason (and there are usually a million ex-cuses), many people don't listen to this voice. But I believe it's crucial that you heed it, or at least try your very hardest to. God is speaking to you. What's right for you is not only speaking from your mind, but from your soul and from your heart. Even if you can't do exactly what you want to do, aim for something that's in the direction of your pas-sion. It could lead you to what you are hoping for. Never give up hope that it will.

A lot of folks have no choice but to work at soul-sucking jobs, because they need the money. Believe me, I took some pretty dreary gigs that did nothing for me but pay my bills so I could keep a roof over my head. That's why I know it's not always easy to aim higher when it comes to work. But once you set your sights on a meaningful goal, you can put yourself on the path. That's the only way higher can be reached—by moving toward it.

A long time ago someone told me, "If you do what you love, you never work a day in your life." In my eyes, there's no truer saying. When you love your work, it doesn't feel like work. It doesn't tax you. It's not overwhelming. It's not a burden. It's something you absolutely, wholeheartedly love.

The first step is to figure out what your meaningful work might be. One way to begin is by describing yourself using only five words. What's the point? Well, understanding who you are and what you value most in life is essential. Like most things, you need to look inward before you can move outward.

While you're examining yourself, pay attention to what gives you the most pleasure during a typical day. Is it writing in your journal? Cooking? Gardening? Speaking with friends? Reading? Spending time with children? Maybe when you go into someone's home, you can't stop re-arranging the furniture in your head. We gravitate toward our strengths.

Also, and this is important, keep purpose in your equation. If you want to find meaningful work, don't focus on only what you love. Think about what you can do to *serve* the people you love.

What stops us from opting for meaningful? We all have self-limiting beliefs; fear of failure is usually the biggest. It can halt you in your tracks. To fight fear or insecurity, hold on to the truth that making the choice to do what you always felt you wanted to do means you're walking into a higher place. You're walking into your destiny, and destiny is always higher than where you are right now.

Then ask yourself: "What would I do if I knew there was no way I could fail?"

Philippians 4:13 (NKJV) says:

I can do all things through Christ who strengthens me.

I love this line of scripture. It tells me that whatever I set my mind to do and whatever I set out to do, I can achieve. I'll have the strength through God. I'll have the force through Christ to make this happen.

As will you.

• What's one small thing you can do today to move yourself forward toward meaningful work?

48

Staying in the Climb

WHILE THE SUN was casting slivers of light through an azure sky, I was laboring up a mountain in Maui with a good friend. I'm not exactly a gazelle, so along the way I had to look down at my feet to be sure of my footing. From time to time, I'd have to catch my breath because of the increasing altitude and thinning air.

At times, when the ground was clear and level, I could take big steps and make real progress. But on difficult inclines, all I could do was manage small, slow steps. The terrain in places was uneven and rough, filled with tangled tree roots, rocks, and ridges. It required plenty of physical effort and focus not to trip. At some point I felt a nagging tiredness like a tug on my sleeve. I just wanted to turn back.

But I pushed on.

Finally, we reached a peak and I thought, "Great. I'm here! Now we can rest." But in a New York minute (or rather an "aloha moment"), I realized that just because I had touched the top of one peak, it didn't mean I had arrived. This wasn't our destination. There were more valleys to traverse and greater heights to reach. In fact, in order to go higher, we often had to descend first—on and on—down and then up again. Time dragged.

Boy, did I want to sit and rest. But my gung ho friend said, "Come on, let's go a little higher." Well, my competitive nature kicked in and bumped up my resolve. I dug in my hiking boots and gave myself a push. Higher we went.

Finally, when we had reached one of the highest points on the mountain, my friend said, "Tyler, this is the best part. Now . . . turn around."

Oh! Wow!

The expansive vista fully enveloped my soul. In more than forty years on this awesome earth, I'd never seen anything as exquisite and bountiful as what I saw in that moment. I was suddenly deeply stilled, as if struck silent by a bolt of electric beauty. The Hawaiian Islands leapt from their glittery silver sea and stretched up to catch the dust of the sky. The clouds were so close I felt I could catch them in my hand. Rays of sunlight danced through the puffs, trying to find a path to show off their power and glow. No artist could do justice to the canvas that was before me. The heavens declared the glory of God. I saw Him in motion.

After several deep breaths of the pure, fresh air, I asked my friend, "When did we get this high?"

"I don't know," she said, beaming. "I was in the climb."

Her response brought me to reverence and to thinking about life. Memories rushed at me full force, like an ocean wave. I thought about how difficult it had been for me, chasing down my dream; how hard it was sometimes to believe in where I was going. I thought about the struggle, the pain, the hope—and the moments when I was plagued by doubt. I remembered the times I was working dead-end jobs, moving through my days with my head down, just taking one step at a time—some small ones, some big ones—wanting to give up, wanting to stop and sit for a while, wanting to wallow in my sorrow, nobody believing in me, nobody thinking it would come to pass, and not realizing that every step was taking me closer to this higher place.

My hike to the Hawaiian mountain peak was painful. Through it all, I was climbing higher, and yet, at the same time, I had no idea how high I was. That's what it's like to chase down a dream.

Sometimes in life, dreams are hard to follow. Just like that climb, you're not aware of how high you're going or if you're even moving. But every step, even when you can't see what's behind you or what's in front of you, brings you closer to your goal. It's in the climb.

You might be struggling right now, but you're in the climb. People may not believe in you, but it's part of the climb. They may take shots at you, but stay in the climb. You may need to stand alone, but you're in the climb. Even if you're not where you want to be right now, I want to say to you what my friend said to me: "This is the best part. Now . . . turn around."

Look how far you've come.
God has brought you here.
You won't be abandoned.
Stay in the climb.

• Consider Proverbs 13:12 (NASB): *Hope deferred makes the heart sick, but desire fulfilled is a tree of life.*

• What can you tell yourself to help you stay in the climb?

• Look back and see how far you've come!

About the Author

Writer, actor, filmmaker, playwright, songwriter, entrepreneur, and philanthropist TYLER PERRY is the mastermind behind nineteen theatrically released feature films, twenty stage plays, nine television shows, and a #1 *New York Times* bestselling book. His creative empire has won over audiences and built communities from the Tyler Perry Studios home base in Atlanta, Georgia, throughout the world. His unique blend of spiritual hope and down-home humor continues to shape his inspiring life story, connecting with fans across the globe and always leaving space to dream. Since 2006, the Perry Foundation's aim has been to transform tragedy into triumph by seeding individual potential, supporting communities, and harvesting real change. The foundation supports education, clean water, health, agriculture, girls' and women's rights, technology, arts, culture, and globally sustainable economic development, both in the United States and around the world.

tylerperry.com
Facebook.com/TylerPerry
Twitter: @tylerperry
Instagram: @tylerperry

About the Type

This book was set in Dante, a typeface designed by Giovanni Mardersteig (1892–1977). Conceived as a private type for the Officina Bodoni in Verona, Italy, Dante was originally cut only for hand composition by Charles Malin, the famous Parisian punch cutter, between 1946 and 1952. Its first use was in an edition of Boccaccio's *Trattatello in laude di Dante* that appeared in 1954. The Monotype Corporation's version of Dante followed in 1957. Though modeled on the Aldine type used for Pietro Cardinal Bembo's treatise *De Aetna* in 1495, Dante is a thoroughly modern interpretation of that venerable face.